# ILLUSTRATED COURSE GUIDES
# Microsoft® PowerPoint® 2010

**Advanced**

# ILLUSTRATED COURSE GUIDES
# Microsoft® PowerPoint® 2010

**Advanced**

David W. Beskeen

COURSE TECHNOLOGY
CENGAGE Learning™

Australia • Brazil • Japan • Korea • Mexico • Singapore • Spain • United Kingdom • United States

## COURSE TECHNOLOGY
### CENGAGE Learning™

**Illustrated Course Guide: Microsoft®
PowerPoint® 2010 Advanced**

David W. Beskeen

Vice President, Publisher: Nicole Jones Pinard

Executive Editor: Marjorie Hunt

Associate Acquisitions Editor: Brandi Shailer

Senior Product Manager: Christina Kling Garrett

Associate Product Manager: Michelle Camisa

Editorial Assistant: Kim Klasner

Director of Marketing: Cheryl Costantini

Senior Marketing Manager: Ryan DeGrote

Marketing Coordinator: Kristen Panciocco

Contributing Author: Carol Cram

Developmental Editors: Rachel Biheller Bunin,
    Pamela Conrad

Content Project Manager: Lisa Weidenfeld

Copy Editor: Mark Goodin

Proofreader: Harold Johnson

Indexer: BIM Indexing and Proofreading Services

QA Manuscript Reviewers: John Frietas, Serge
    Palladino, Susan Pedicini, Jeff Schwartz, Danielle
    Shaw, Marianne Snow

Print Buyer: Fola Orekoya

Cover Designer: GEX Publishing Services

Cover Artist: Mark Hunt

Composition: GEX Publishing Services

Credits:

G-6 Photos courtesy of Donna Goudy, Janet Moffat,
    and Karen Beskeen

H-4 Photo courtesy of Donna Goudy

H-6 Photo courtesy of Janet Moffat

H-14, H-15 Photos courtesy of Barbara Hilliard

H-20 Photos courtesy of Justin Beskeen

H-21 Photos courtesy of Barbara Hilliard and
    Joan Johnson

For product information and technology assistance, contact us at
**Cengage Learning Customer & Sales Support, 1-800-354-9706**

For permission to use material from this text or product, submit all requests online at **www.cengage.com/permissions**
Further permissions questions can be emailed to
**permissionrequest@cengage.com**

Trademarks:

Some of the product names and company names used in this book have been used for identification purposes only and may be trademarks or registered trademarks of their respective manufacturers and sellers.

Microsoft and the Office logo are either registered trademarks or trademarks of Microsoft Corporation in the United States and/or other countries. Course Technology, Cengage Learning is an independent entity from Microsoft Corporation, and not affiliated with Microsoft in any manner.

Library of Congress Control Number: 2010938667

ISBN-13: 978-0-538-74843-8
ISBN-10: 0-538-74843-5

**Course Technology**
20 Channel Center Street
Boston, MA 02210
USA

Cengage Learning is a leading provider of customized learning solutions with office locations around the globe, including Singapore, the United Kingdom, Australia, Mexico, Brazil, and Japan. Locate your local office at:
**international.cengage.com/region**

Cengage Learning products are represented in Canada by Nelson Education, Ltd.

To learn more about Course Technology, visit **www.cengage.com/coursetechnology**

To learn more about Cengage Learning, visit **www.cengage.com**

Purchase any of our products at your local college store or at our preferred online store
**www.cengagebrain.com**

Printed in the United States of America
1 2 3 4 5 6 7 8 9 18 17 16 15 14 13 12 11 10

# Brief Contents

# Contents

# Preface

Welcome to *Illustrated Course Guide: Microsoft® PowerPoint® 2010 Advanced*. If this is your first experience with the Illustrated Course Guides, you'll see that this book has a unique design: each skill is presented on two facing pages, with steps on the left and screens on the right. The layout makes it easy to learn a skill without having to read a lot of text and flip pages to see an illustration.

This book is an ideal learning tool for a wide range of learners—the "rookies" will find the clean design easy to follow and focused with only essential information presented, and the "hotshots" will appreciate being able to move quickly through the lessons to find the information they need without reading a lot of text. The design also makes this a great reference after the course is over! See the illustration on the right to learn more about the pedagogical and design elements of a typical lesson.

## What's New In This Edition

- **Fully Updated.** Highlights the new features of Microsoft PowerPoint 2010 including new 3-D motion slide transitions, artistic effects and textures for pictures, organizing slides into sections, co-authoring capabilities, broadcasting a presentation over the Internet, and the new Backstage view.

- **Maps to SAM 2010.** This book is designed to work with SAM (Skills Assessment Manager) 2010. **SAM Assessment** contains performance-based, hands-on SAM exams for each unit of this book, and **SAM Training** provides hands-on training for skills covered in the book. Some exercises are available in **SAM Projects**, which is auto-grading software that provides both learners and instructors with immediate, detailed feedback (SAM sold separately.) See page xii for more information on SAM.

Each two-page spread focuses on a single skill.

Introduction briefly explains why the lesson skill is important.

A case scenario motivates the the steps and puts learning in context.

Tips and troubleshooting advice, right where you need it—next to the step itself.

### Animating a Chart

**UNIT F** PowerPoint 2010

You can animate elements of a chart, much in the same way you animate text and graphics. You can animate the entire chart as one object, or you can animate the data markers. There are two options for animating data markers individually: by series or by category. Animating data markers individually by series displays data markers of each data series (or the same-colored data markers). Animating data markers individually by category displays the data markers of each category in the chart. If you choose to animate the chart's data markers as a series, the entire data series is animated as a group; the same is true for animating data markers by category. You decide to animate the data series markers of the chart.

**STEPS**

**QUICK TIP**
Exit animation effects cause an object to leave the slide. To add an exit animation, open the Animation gallery, then select an effect in the Exit section.

1. Verify that the chart is selected, click the Animations tab on the Ribbon, click the More button in the Animation group, then click Random Bars
   The Random Bars entrance animation is applied to the entire chart, and PowerPoint plays the animation.

2. Click the Animation Pane button in the Advanced Animation group, then click the Content Placeholder 8 list arrow
   The Animation Pane opens and displays specific information, such as the type of animation (Entrance, Exit, Emphasis, or Motion Path), the sequence and timeline of the animation, and the name of the animated object. Clicking an animation's list arrow provides access to other custom options. Compare your screen to Figure F-9.

3. Click in the Animation group, click Fly In, then click the Duration up arrow in the Timing group until 1.00 appears
   The Fly In entrance animation replaces the Random Bars entrance animation. A longer duration, or animation timing, slows down the animation.

**QUICK TIP**
If you don't want to animate the chart background, click the animation list arrow in the Animation Pane, click Effect Options, click the Chart Animation tab, then remove the check in the check box.

4. Click the Effect Options button in the Animation group, point to each option in the Direction and Sequence sections of the gallery and watch the Live Preview of the animation, then click By Elements in Series in the Sequence section
   Each data series marker, by series, flies in from the left of the slide beginning with the Standard Rail data series. There are now 13 animation tags, one for the chart background and one for each data series marker.

5. Click the Expand contents arrow in the Animation Pane, click the first animation tag 1 on the slide, click Fade in the Animation group, then click the Duration up arrow until 1.50 appears
   The Fade animation is now applied to the chart background. Notice the timeline icon for the chart background animation is wider to account for the longer duration.

6. Click the Play button in the Animation Pane, then watch all the animations
   The chart background fades into view, then data series markers fly in from the left one after another. Notice the advancing timeline (vertical blue line) as it moves over each animation in the Animation Pane.

**QUICK TIP**
Due to the large number of animation options available with charts and other objects, be careful how many objects you animate on one slide.

7. Click the Hide contents arrow in the Animation Pane, click the Delay up arrow until .50 appears, then click the Play button in the Animation Pane
   A half second delay is applied between each animation. Watch closely at how the changed settings affect the progression of the animated data series markers.

8. Click the Start list arrow in the Timing group, click After Previous, click the Trigger button in the Advanced Animation group, point to On Click of, then click Title 1
   Now when Slide 11 appears in Slide Show view, you can click the slide title to play the chart animations. The animation tags combine into one lightning bolt tag indicating the animation has a trigger.

9. Click the Slide Show button on the status bar, click the slide title, watch the animation, press [Esc], close the Animation Pane, then save the presentation
   Compare your screen to Figure F-10.

PowerPoint 130    Enhancing Charts

Large screen shots keep learners on track as they complete steps

Brightly colored tabs indicate which section of the book you are in.

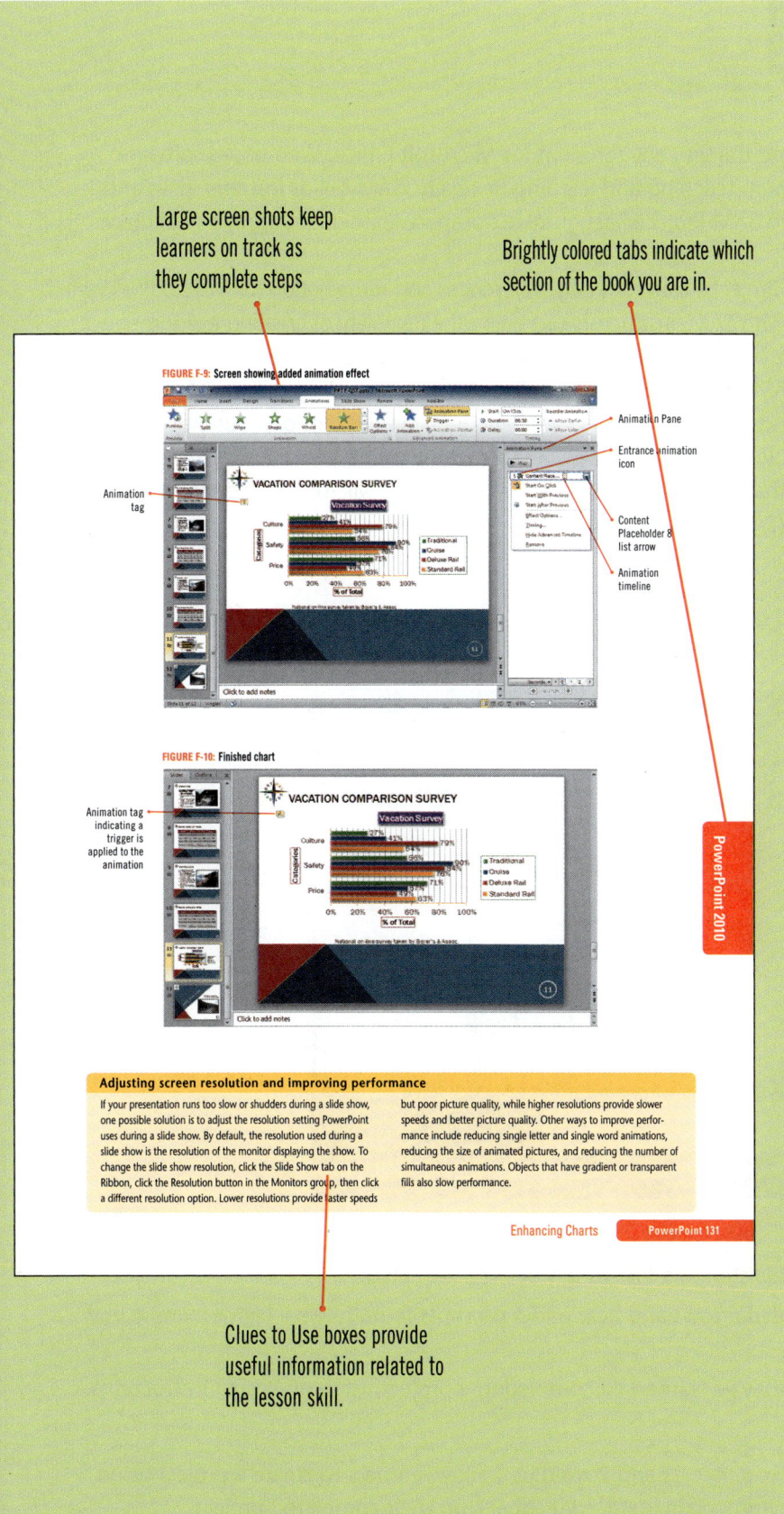

Clues to Use boxes provide useful information related to the lesson skill.

## Assignments

The lessons use Quest Specialty Travel, a fictional adventure travel company, as the case study. The assignments on the light yellow pages at the end of each unit increase in difficulty. Assignments include:

- **Concepts Review** consist of multiple choice, matching, and screen identification questions.

- **Skills Reviews** are hands-on, step-by-step exercises that review the skills covered in each lesson in the unit.

- **Independent Challenges** are case projects requiring critical thinking and application of the unit skills. The Independent Challenges increase in difficulty, with the first one in each unit being the easiest. Independent Challenges 2 and 3 become increasingly open-ended, requiring more independent problem solving.

- **Real Life Independent Challenges** are practical exercises in which learners create documents to help them with their every day lives.

- **Advanced Challenge Exercises** set within the Independent Challenges provide optional steps for more advanced learners.

- **Visual Workshops** are practical, self-graded capstone projects that require independent problem solving.

# About SAM

SAM is the premier proficiency-based assessment and training environment for Microsoft Office. Web-based software along with an inviting user interface provide maximum teaching and learning flexibility. SAM builds learners' skills and confidence with a variety of real-life simulations, and SAM Projects' assignments prepare learners for today's workplace.

The SAM system includes Assessment, Training, and Projects, featuring page references and remediation for this book as well as Course Technology's Microsoft Office textbooks. With SAM, instructors can enjoy the flexibility of creating assignments based on content from their favorite Microsoft Office books or based on specific course objectives. Instructors appreciate the scheduling and reporting options that have made SAM the market-leading online testing and training software for over a decade. Over 2,000 performance-based questions and matching Training simulations, as well as tens of thousands of objective-based questions from many Course Technology texts, provide instructors with a variety of choices across multiple applications. SAM Projects is auto-grading software that lets learners complete projects using Microsoft Office and then receive detailed feedback on their finished projects. (SAM sold separately)

## SAM Assessment

- Content for these hands-on, performance-based tasks includes Word, Excel, Access, PowerPoint, Internet Explorer, Outlook, and Windows. Includes tens of thousands of objective-based questions from many Course Technology texts.

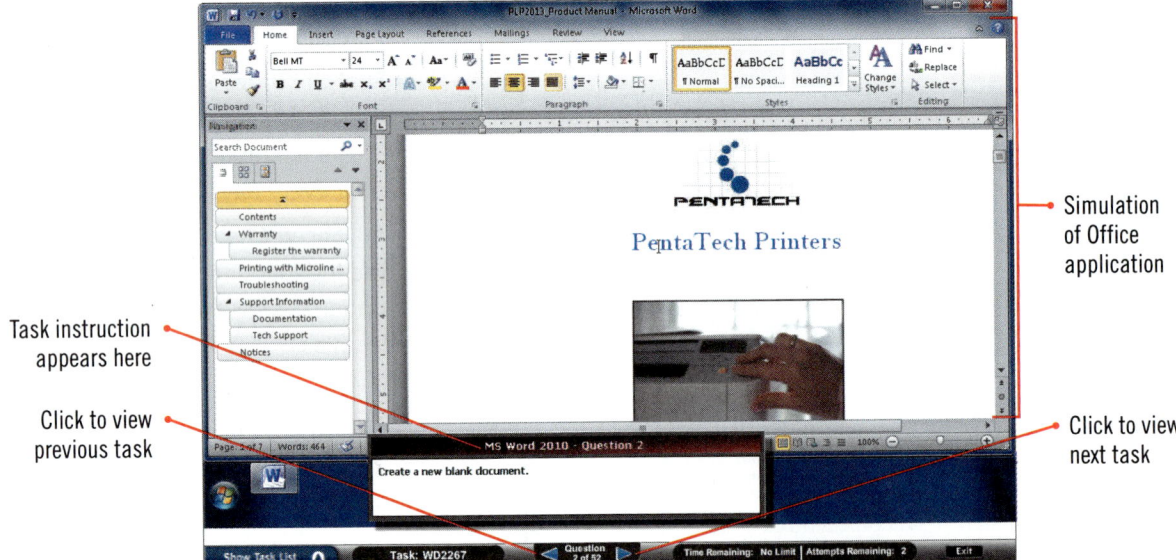

Task instruction appears here

Click to view previous task

Simulation of Office application

Click to view next task

## SAM Training

- Observe mode allows the learners to watch and listen to a task as it is being completed.
- Practice mode allows the learner to follow guided arrows and hear audio prompts to help visual learners know how to complete a task.
- Apply mode allows the learner to prove what they've learned by completing a project using on-screen instructions.

## SAM Projects

- Live-in-the-application assignments in Word, Excel, Access and PowerPoint allow learners to create a project using the Microsoft Office software and then receive immediate, detailed feedback on their completed project.
- Learners receive detailed feedback on their project within minutes.
- Unique anti-cheating detection feature is encrypted into the data files to ensure learners complete their own assignments.

# Instructor Resources

The Instructor Resources CD is Course Technology's way of putting the resources and information needed to teach and learn effectively into your hands. With an integrated array of teaching and learning tools that offer you and your learners a broad range of technology-based instructional options, we believe this CD represents the highest quality and most cutting edge resources available to instructors today. The resources available with this book are:

- **Instructor's Manual**—Available as an electronic file, the Instructor's Manual includes detailed lecture topics with teaching tips for each unit.

- **Sample Syllabus**—Prepare and customize your course easily using this sample course outline.

- **PowerPoint Presentations**—Each unit has a corresponding PowerPoint presentation that you can use in lecture, distribute to your learners, or customize to suit your course.

- **Figure Files**—The figures in the text are provided on the Instructor Resources CD to help you illustrate key topics or concepts. You can create traditional overhead transparencies by printing the figure files. Or you can create electronic slide shows by using the figures in a presentation program such as PowerPoint.

- **Solutions to Exercises**—Solutions to Exercises contains every file learners are asked to create or modify in the lessons and end-of-unit material. Also provided in this section, there is a document outlining the solutions for the end-of-unit Concepts Review, Skills Review, and Independent Challenges. An Annotated Solution File and Grading Rubric accompany each file and can be used together for quick and easy grading.

- **Data Files for Learners**—To complete most of the units in this book, learners will need Data Files. You can post the Data Files on a file server for learners to copy. The Data Files are available on the Instructor Resources CD-ROM, the Review Pack, and can also be downloaded from cengagebrain.com. For more information on how to download the Data Files, see the inside back cover.

Instruct learners to use the Data Files List included on the Review Pack and the Instructor Resources CD. This list gives instructions on copying and organizing files.

- **ExamView**—ExamView is a powerful testing software package that allows you to create and administer printed, computer (LAN-based), and Internet exams. ExamView includes hundreds of questions that correspond to the topics covered in this text, enabling learners to generate detailed study guides that include page references for further review. The computer-based and Internet testing components allow learners to take exams at their computers, and also saves you time by grading each exam automatically.

## Content for Online Learning.

Course Technology has partnered with the leading distance learning solution providers and class-management platforms today. To access this material, visit www.cengage.com/webtutor and search for your title. Instructor resources include the following: additional case projects, sample syllabi, PowerPoint presentations, and more. For additional information, please contact your sales representative. For learners to access this material, they must have purchased a WebTutor PIN-code specific to this title and your campus platform. The resources for learners might include (based on instructor preferences): topic reviews, review questions, practice tests, and more.

# Acknowledgements

## Instructor Advisory Board

We thank our Instructor Advisory Board who gave us their opinions and guided our decisions as we updated our texts for Microsoft Office 2010. They are as follows:

**Terri Helfand**, Chaffey Community College

**Barbara Comfort**, J. Sargeant Reynolds Community College

**Brenda Nielsen**, Mesa Community College

**Sharon Cotman**, Thomas Nelson Community College

**Marian Meyer**, Central New Mexico Community College

**Audrey Styer**, Morton College

**Richard Alexander**, Heald College

**Xiaodong Qiao**, Heald College

## Student Advisory Board

We also thank our Student Advisory Board members, who shared their experiences using the book and offered suggestions to make it better: **Latasha Jefferson**, Thomas Nelson Community College, **Gary Williams**, Thomas Nelson Community College, **Stephanie Miller**, J. Sargeant Reynolds Community College, **Sarah Styer**, Morton Community College, **Missy Marino**, Chaffey College

## Author Acknowledgements

**David W. Beskeen** Being a part of the extremely talented and experienced Office Illustrated team makes working on this book that much more enjoyable—many thanks to Rachel Biheller Bunin, Christina Kling Garrett, the production group, the testers, and the rest of the Cengage team! I also want to acknowledge my family, especially my parents Don and Darlene, for all they have done for me...I am forever grateful.

## Dedication

This book is dedicated to the memory of Donald W. Beskeen

# Read This Before You Begin

## Frequently Asked Questions

### What are Data Files?

A Data File is a partially completed PowerPoint presentation or another type of file that you use to complete the steps in the units and exercises to create the final document that you submit to your instructor. Each unit opener page lists the Data Files that you need for that unit.

### Where are the Data Files?

Your instructor will provide the Data Files to you or direct you to a location on a network drive from which you can download them. For information on how to download the Data Files from cengagebrain.com, see the inside back cover.

### What software was used to write and test this book?

This book was written and tested using a typical installation of Microsoft Office 2010 Professional Plus on a computer with a typical installation of Microsoft Windows 7 Ultimate.

The browser used for any Web-dependent steps is Internet Explorer 8.

### Do I need to be connected to the Internet to complete the steps and exercises in this book?

Some of the exercises in this book require that your computer be connected to the Internet. If you are not connected to the Internet, see your instructor for information on how to complete the exercises.

### What do I do if my screen is different from the figures shown in this book?

This book was written and tested on computers with monitors set at a resolution of $1024 \times 768$. If your screen shows more or less information than the figures in the book, your monitor is probably set at a higher or lower resolution. If you don't see something on your screen, you might have to scroll down or up to see the object identified in the figures.

The Ribbon—the blue area at the top of the screen—in Microsoft Office 2010 adapts to different resolutions. If your monitor is set at a lower resolution than $1024 \times 768$, you might not see all of the buttons shown in the figures. The groups of buttons will always appear, but the entire group might be condensed into a single button that you need to click to access the buttons described in the instructions.

**COURSECASTS** Learning on the Go. Always Available...Always Relevant.

Our fast-paced world is driven by technology. You know because you are an active participant—always on the go, always keeping up with technological trends, and always learning new ways to embrace technology to power your life. Let CourseCasts, hosted by Ken Baldauf of Florida State University, be your guide into weekly updates in this ever-changing space. These timely, relevant podcasts are produced weekly and are available for download at http://coursecasts.course.com or directly from iTunes (search by CourseCasts). CourseCasts are a perfect solution to getting learners (and even instructors) to learn on the go!

# Enhancing Charts

A PowerPoint presentation is first and foremost a visual communication tool. Slides that deliver information with relevant graphics have a more lasting impact on an audience than slides with plain text. The most effective way to display numerical data is to show the data graphically in a chart. You can show numerical data in many different ways including columns, bars, lines, or pie wedges. When choosing a chart type, it is important to consider which type of chart best illustrates your data. For example, a pie chart is designed to display data from one data series in proportion to the sum of all the data series; whereas, a column chart is designed to display data changes over time or for demonstrating comparisons among data points. In this unit, you continue to work on the Quest Specialty Travel (QST) presentation that includes charts. You customize the chart layout, format chart elements, and animate the chart. Finally, you embed an Excel chart, and then you link an Excel worksheet to the presentation.

## OBJECTIVES

Work with charts in PowerPoint

Change chart design and style

Customize a chart layout

Format chart elements

Animate a chart

Embed an Excel chart

Link an Excel worksheet

Update a linked Excel worksheet

# Working with Charts in PowerPoint

One of the best ways to enhance a presentation is to insert graphic elements such as a chart. When you have numerical data that you want to compare, a chart helps the audience visualize and understand the information. Because Excel is integrated with PowerPoint, you can easily create fantastic-looking charts on the presentation slides. As you continue to develop the QST presentation, you plan to include charts on several slides. You review the features, benefits, and methods of charting in PowerPoint.

## DETAILS

**QUICK TIP**

If you open a presentation with a chart that was created in Microsoft Graph, PowerPoint recognizes it and allows you to open and edit it using Excel.

- ### Create charts using Excel from within PowerPoint

  If you have Microsoft Office 2010 installed on your computer, PowerPoint uses Excel, by default, to create charts. When you create a chart using the Chart button in PowerPoint, a sample chart is placed on the slide and a separate Excel window opens beside the PowerPoint window displaying the chart's data in a worksheet. Displaying both program windows at the same time provides you with the ability to work directly on the chart in the Excel window and see the changes on the slide in the PowerPoint window. See Figure F-1. If you don't have Excel, Microsoft Graph opens and displays a chart and a datasheet where you can enter your own data.

- ### Embed or link a chart

  You have some options to choose from when inserting an Excel chart to your presentation. There are two ways to add a chart to a slide: you can embed it or link it. An embedded chart is an object created in another program and inserted in a slide. An embedded chart becomes a part of the presentation like a picture or a piece of clip art. The embedded chart's data is stored in an Excel worksheet that is included with the presentation file. You can embed a chart in PowerPoint using the Chart button on the Insert tab or by copying a chart from Excel and pasting it on a slide. A linked chart is also created in another program, but it is saved in a separate file and not with the presentation. If you want to make changes to a linked Excel chart, you must open the saved Excel file that contains the chart.

**QUICK TIP**

A chart template does not save theme or style information, only chart type information.

- ### Modify charts using styles and layouts

  Because themes and theme effects are alike for all Office programs, you can apply a specific theme or effect to a chart in Excel, and PowerPoint will recognize the theme or effect. Using themes gives your chart a consistent look with other objects in your presentation; however, you can fine-tune individual elements, such as the data series or legend of your chart. In addition, there are a number of chart layouts that you can apply to your chart. A chart layout specifies where chart elements, such as axes titles, data labels, and the legend, are displayed within the chart area. You cannot create your own chart layouts and styles, but you can create a template of a customized chart, which you can use later to apply to another chart.

**QUICK TIP**

If you do not have Excel 2010 installed on your computer, you cannot use any of the advanced charting capabilities in Microsoft Office 2010.

- ### Add advanced formatting to charts

  If the basic predefined chart styles do not provide you with the formatting options you want, you can choose to modify individual elements. For example, you may want to alter the way data labels look or how axes are displayed. You can specify the axes scales and adjust the interval between the values or categories. You can also add trendlines and error bars to a chart to provide more information about the data. A **trendline** is a graphical representation of an upward or downward trend in a data series, also used to predict future trends. **Error bars** identify potential error amounts relative to each data marker in a data series. Figure F-2 displays some advanced formatting items.

PowerPoint window

Excel window

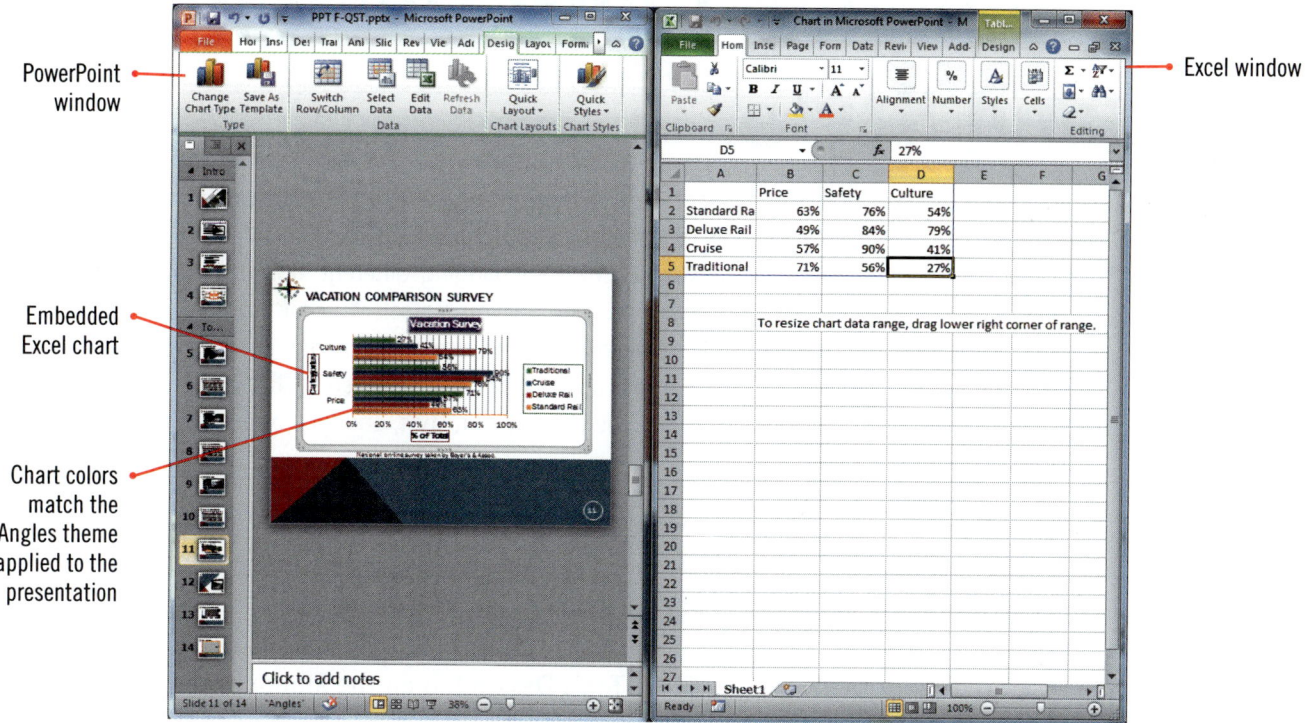

Embedded Excel chart

Chart colors match the Angles theme applied to the presentation

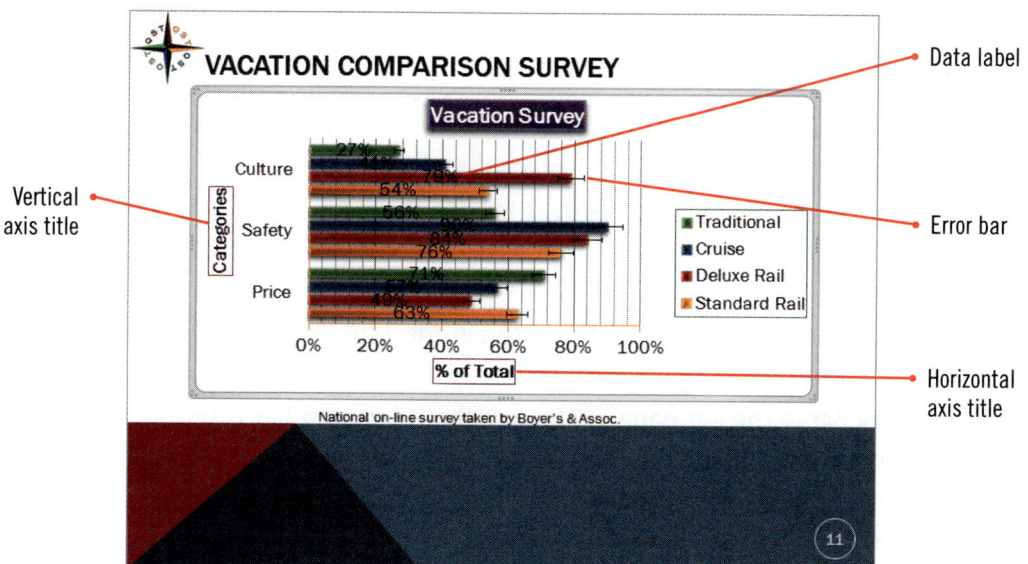

Data label

Vertical axis title

Error bar

Horizontal axis title

## Changing page setup and slide orientation

When you need to customize the size and orientation of the slides in your presentation, you can do so using the commands in the Page Setup group on the Design tab on the Ribbon. Click the Page Setup button to open the Page Setup dialog box. In the Page Setup dialog box, you can change the width and height of the slides to 12 different settings, including On-screen Show, Letter Paper, 35mm Slides, and Banner. You can also set a custom slide size by determining the height and width of the slides. If the presentation would work better in Portrait rather than Landscape mode, you can set the slide orientation in the Page Setup dialog box by clicking the Slide Orientation option button in the Slides section. The orientation setting for the slides is separate from the orientation setting for the notes, handouts, and outline. To change slide orientation of the presentation from the Ribbon, click the Slide Orientation button in the Page Setup group on the Design tab.

# Changing Chart Design and Style

Being able to use Excel to create charts in PowerPoint offers you many advantages, including the ability to format charts using Excel Chart tools to customize the design, layout, and formatting. After you create a chart, you can immediately alter the way it looks by changing different individual chart elements or by applying a predefined chart layout or style. For example, you can select a chart layout that adds a chart title and moves the legend to the bottom of the chart. You can also easily change the color and effects of chart elements by applying one of the styles found in the Chart Styles gallery.  The chart that includes survey results needs some work. You change the chart layout, style, and type of the chart on Slide 11.

**STEPS**

1. **Start PowerPoint, open the presentation PPT F-1.pptx from the drive and folder where you store your Data Files, save the presentation as PPT F-QST, then click the Slide 11 thumbnail in the Slides tab**

   Slide 11 appears in the Slide pane.

2. **Click the chart, then click the Chart Tools Design tab on the Ribbon**

   The chart is selected and ready to edit.

3. **Click the More button ⬇ in the Chart Layouts group, then click Layout 9 in the Layout gallery**

   This particular layout option adds a chart title and value and category axis titles to the chart, as shown in Figure F-3.

4. **Click Chart Title, type Vacation Survey, click Vertical (Value) Axis Title, type % of Total, click Horizontal (Category) Axis Title, type Categories, then click in a blank area of the chart**

   The new chart labels help identify aspects of the chart.

5. **Click the More button ⬇ in the Chart Styles group, then click Style 18**

   The Style 18 option removes some shading and dark colors to make the chart easier to read. This new style option also adds a light outline to the data series markers, for better contrast between the markers.

6. **Click the Change Chart Type button in the Type group**

   The Change Chart Type dialog box opens.

7. **Click Bar in the left pane, make sure that Clustered Bar is selected, then click OK**

   The data series markers change from columns to bars and rotate 90 degrees. Notice also that the value and category axis have switched places with this new chart type. Compare your screen to Figure F-4.

8. **Click a blank area of the slide, then save your presentation**

**FIGURE F-3:** Chart showing new layout

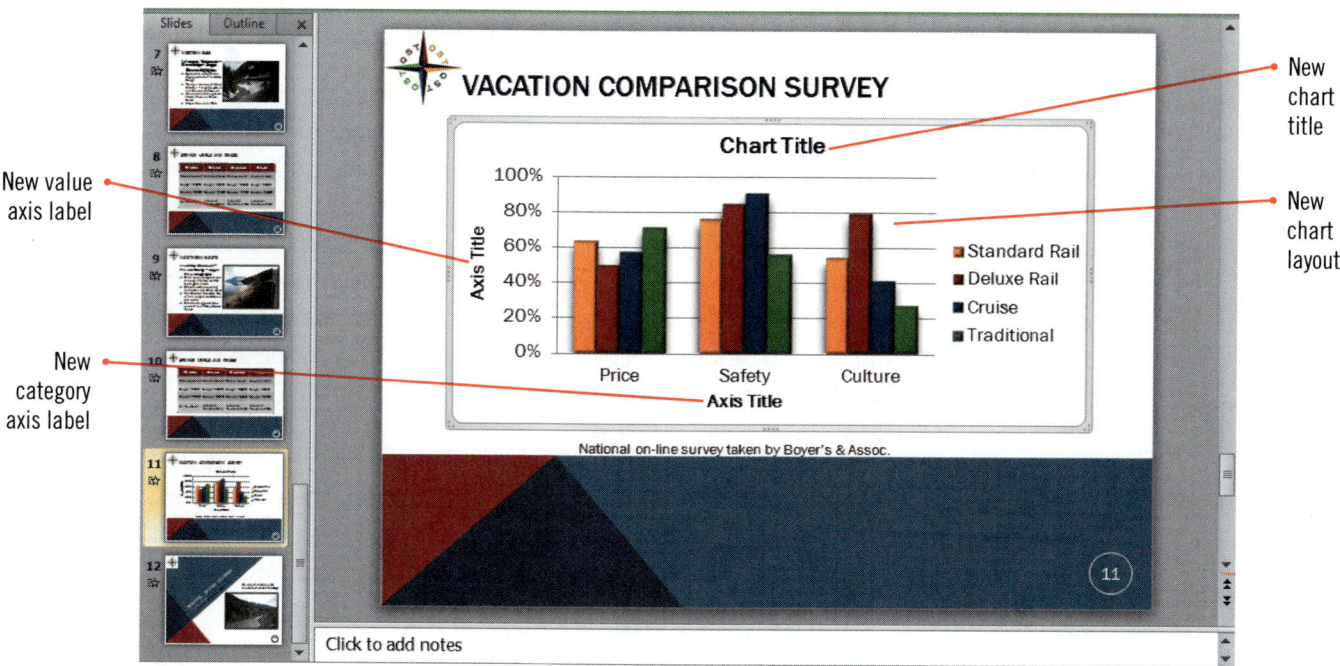

New value axis label

New category axis label

New chart title

New chart layout

**FIGURE F-4:** Chart showing new style and axis labels

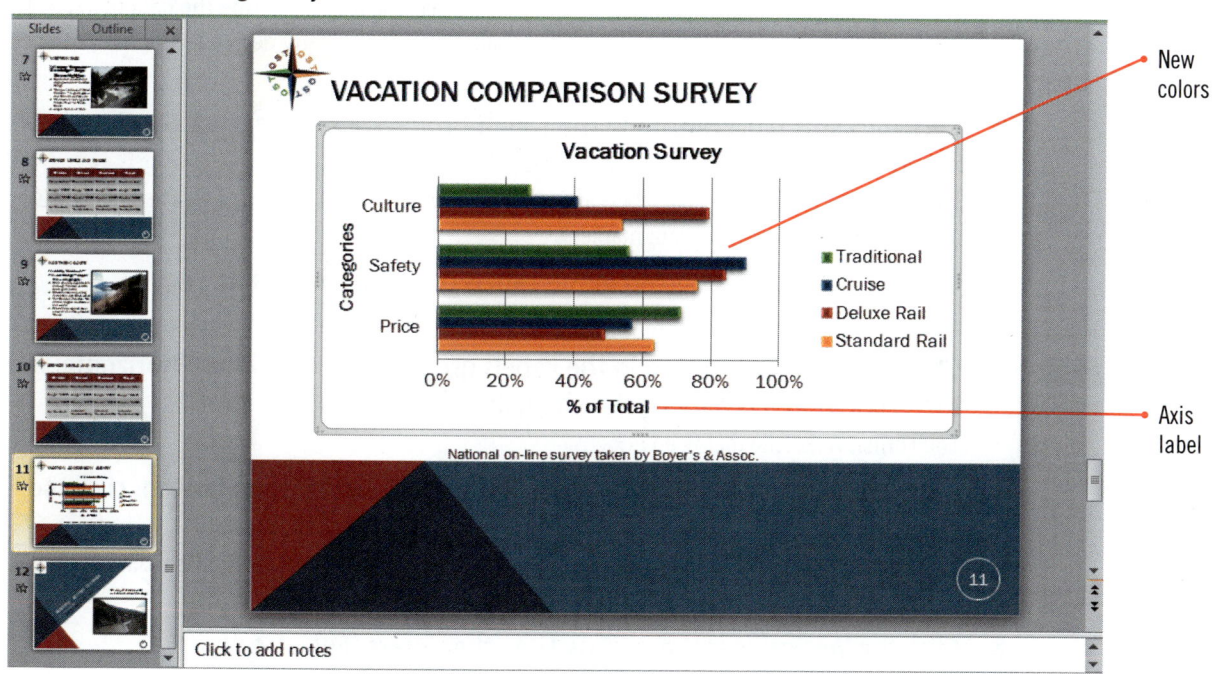

New colors

Axis label

PowerPoint 2010

## Saving a chart as a template

If you create a customized chart that you want to reuse, you can save it as a template (*.crtx) to the Charts Template folder. A chart template stores the formatting and layout of a chart. Then, instead of re-creating the chart type, you simply apply the chart template to an existing chart or create a new chart based on the template. To save a chart as a template, select the chart you want to save, then click the Save As Template button in the Type group on the Chart Tools Design tab. To apply a chart template to an existing chart, click the Change Chart Type button in the Type group, click Templates, then click the chart template.

# Customizing a Chart Layout

One of the many advantages of using Excel to create charts in PowerPoint is the ability you have to customize chart elements, such as labels, axes, gridlines, and the chart background. For example, you can change the plot area color so the data markers are distinctly set off, or you can add gridlines to a chart. Gridlines help make the data easier to read in the chart and extend from the horizontal axis or the vertical axis across the plot area. There are two types of gridlines: major gridlines and minor gridlines. **Major gridlines** identify major units on the axis and are usually identified by a tick mark. **Tick marks** are small lines of measurement that intersect an axis and identify the categories, values, or series in a chart. **Minor gridlines** identify minor units on the axis and can also be identified by a tick mark.  You decide to improve the appearance of the chart by customizing some elements of the chart.

1. **Click the chart, click the Chart Tools Layout tab on the Ribbon, then click the Gridlines button in the Axes group**

   The Gridlines menu opens. The chart already has major gridlines on the vertical axis.

2. **Point to Primary Vertical Gridlines, then click Major & Minor Gridlines**

   This adds minor vertical gridlines to the chart as shown in Figure F-5. Notice that the major gridlines are darker in color than the minor gridlines and are identified by a tick mark on the value axis at each unit of value.

3. **Click the Data Table button in the Labels group, then click Show Data Table with Legend Keys**

   You like seeing the data displayed in the data table because it helps define the data markers. However, using the data table takes up too much room on the slide and significantly decreases the size of the chart making it unreadable.

4. **Click the Data Table button in the Labels group, click None, click the Data Labels button in the Labels group, then click Center**

   The data table closes, and data labels appear in the center of each data marker. The data labels are a little hard to read in the center of the data markers.

5. **Click the Data Labels button in the Labels group, click Outside End**

   The data labels move to the end of the data markers.

6. **Click the Axis Titles button in the Labels group, point to Primary Horizontal Axis Title, then click More Primary Horizontal Axis Title Options**

   The Format Axis Title dialog box opens.

7. **Click Border Color in the left pane, click the Solid line option button, click the Color list arrow [icon], click Red, Accent 2 in the top row, then click Close**

   A dark red border appears around the value axis title. The category axis title would also look good with a border around it.

8. **Click the Vertical (Category) Axis Title, then press [F4]**

   A dark red border appears around the category axis title. Pressing [F4] repeats the last formatting action.

9. **Click a blank area of the slide, then save your presentation**

   Compare your screen to Figure F-6.

**FIGURE F-5:** Chart showing new minor gridlines

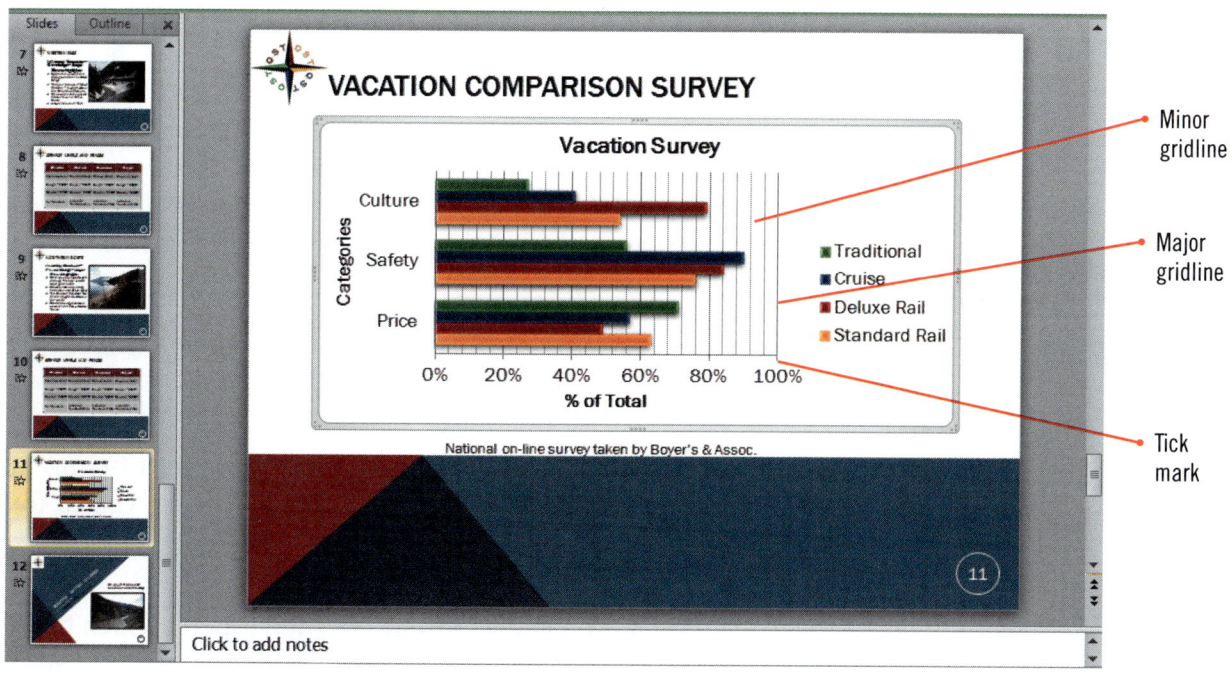

Minor gridline

Major gridline

Tick mark

**FIGURE F-6:** Chart showing added and formatted elements

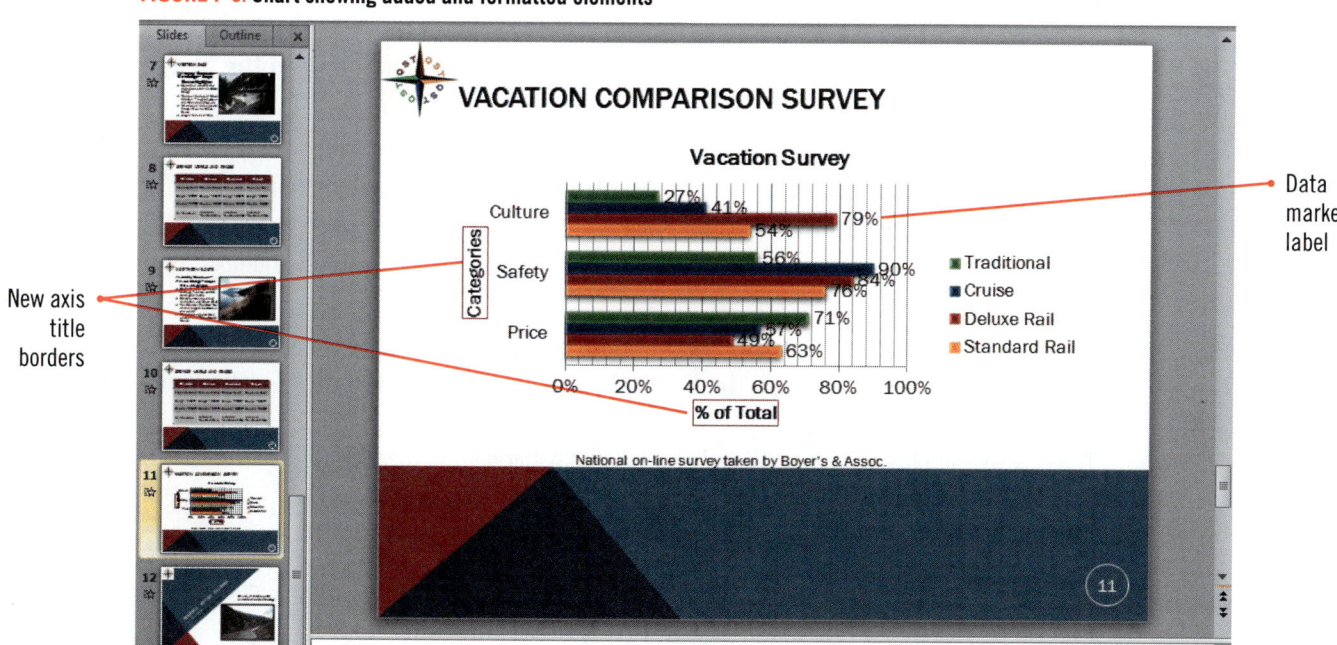

New axis title borders

Data marker label

PowerPoint 2010

## Using the Research task pane

Sometimes when you are developing a presentation, you need help formulating your ideas or researching a subject. PowerPoint has an extensive set of online tools found in the Research task pane that gives you immediate access to many different kinds of information. The Research task pane provides the following research tools: an English dictionary; an English, French, and Spanish thesaurus; a word and phrase translator; three research Web sites; and two business research Web sites. To open the Research task pane, click the Research button in the Proofing group on the Review tab. The Research options link at the bottom of the Research task pane provides additional research books and research sites that you can add to the Research task pane.

# Formatting Chart Elements

Quick Styles in PowerPoint provide you with a number of choices to modify all the elements in a chart. Even with all the Quick Style choices, you still may want to format individual elements to make the chart easy to read and understand. 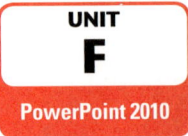 Overall, you like what you have done to the vacation survey chart so far, but you decide to format some individual elements of the chart to better fit the QST presentation design. You also consider using the copy and paste commands for inserting other charts on a slide.

## STEPS

**QUICK TIP**
You can also click a data marker in the chart to select all of the data series markers.

1. **Click a blank area in the Chart, click the Chart Tools Layout tab on the Ribbon, click the Chart Area list arrow in the Current Selection group, then click Series "Standard Rail"**
   All of the Standard Rail data markers are selected in the chart.

2. **Click the Chart Tools Format tab on the Ribbon, click the Shape Fill list arrow in the Shape Styles group, point to Gradient, then click Linear Diagonal – Bottom Left to Top Right in the Dark Variations section (bottom row)**
   The Standard Rail data series markers change to gradient fill.

3. **Click the Format Selection button in the Current Selection group to open the Format Data Series dialog box, drag the Series Overlap slider to the left towards Separated until –50% appears in the Series Overlap text box, then click Close**
   A small space is applied between the data markers for each data series in the chart. You can enter a value from –100 percent to 100 percent in the Series Overlap text box. A negative number adds space between each data marker, and a positive number overlaps the data markers. Compare your screen to Figure F-7.

4. **Click the Vacation Survey chart title, then click the More button ⊡ in the Shape Styles group**
   The Shapes Style gallery opens.

5. **Click Moderate Effect – Dark Purple, Accent 5 (5th row), then click any one of the numbers on the Horizontal (Value) Axis**
   Applying the new style to the chart title makes it stand out. Clicking any of the numbers on the value axis selects the entire axis.

6. **Click the More button ⊡ in the Shape Styles group, click Subtle Line – Accent 1 (1st row), click any one of the words on the Vertical (Category) Axis, then click Subtle Line – Accent 1 in the Shape Styles group**
   The new style applies an orange color to the axis and better defines the plot area.

7. **Right-click the chart legend, then click Format Legend in the shortcut menu**
   The Format Legend dialog box opens.

8 **Click Border Color in the left pane, click the Solid line option button, click the Color list arrow ⬙ ▾, click Dark Green, Accent 4 (top row), then click Close**
   A solid dark green border line appears around the legend.

9. **Click a blank area of the slide, then save the presentation**
   Compare your screen to Figure F-8.

**FIGURE F-7:** Chart showing modified data markers

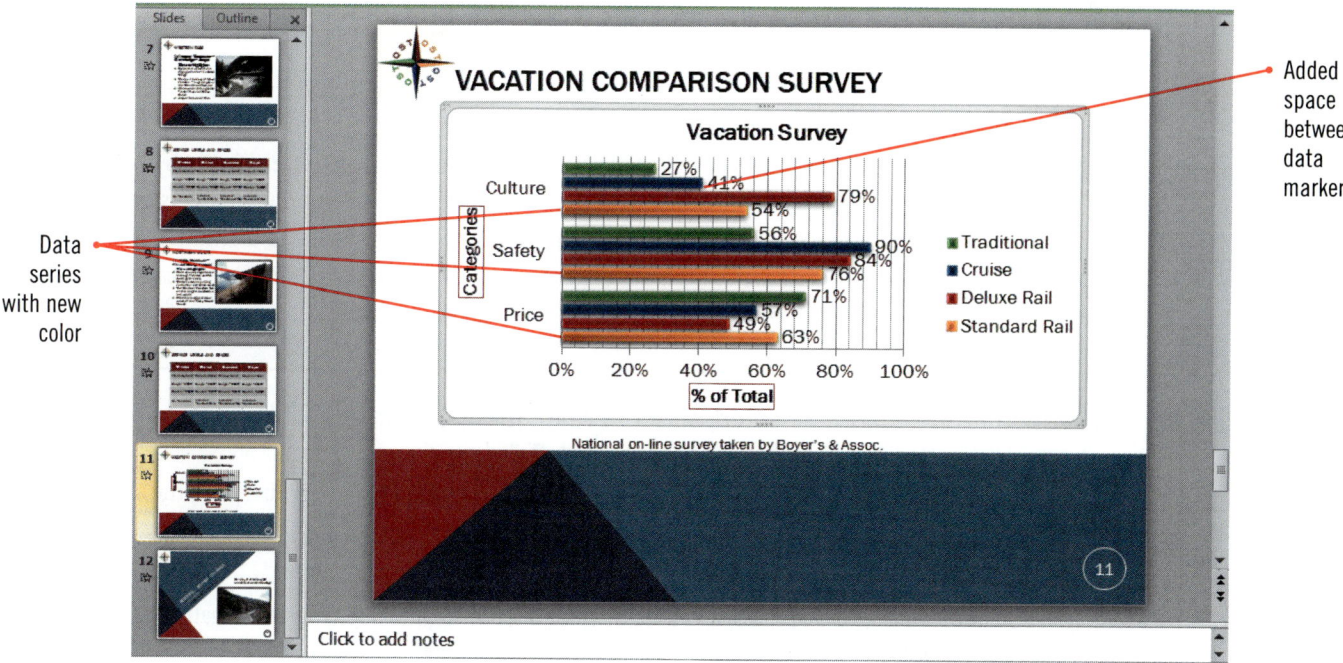

**FIGURE F-8:** Completed chart

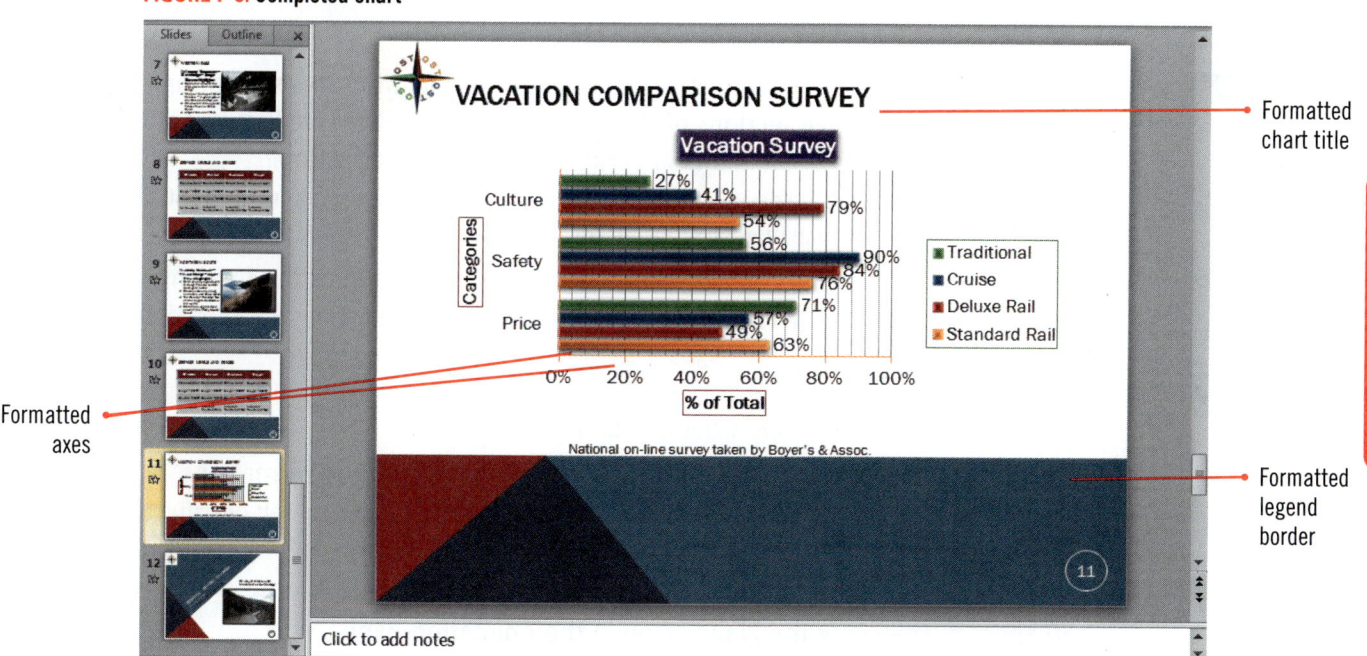

## Changing PowerPoint options

You can customize your installation of PowerPoint by changing various settings and preferences. To change PowerPoint settings, click the File tab on the Ribbon, then click Options to open the PowerPoint Options dialog box. In the dialog box there are nine sections identified in the left pane, which offer you ways to customize PowerPoint. For example, the General area includes options for viewing the Mini toolbar, enabling Live Preview, and personalizing your copy of Office.

# Animating a Chart

You can animate elements of a chart, much in the same way you animate text and graphics. You can animate the entire chart as one object, or you can animate the data markers. There are two options for animating data markers individually: by series or by category. Animating data markers individually by series displays data markers of each data series (or the same-colored data markers). Animating data markers individually by category displays the data markers of each category in the chart. If you choose to animate the chart's data markers as a series, the entire data series is animated as a group; the same is true for animating data markers by category. You decide to animate the data series markers of the chart.

## STEPS

1. **Verify that the chart is selected, click the Animations tab on the Ribbon, click the More button ⬇ in the Animation group, then click Random Bars**

   The Random Bars entrance animation is applied to the entire chart, and PowerPoint plays the animation.

2. **Click the Animation Pane button in the Advanced Animation group, then click the Content Placeholder 8 list arrow**

   The Animation Pane opens and displays specific information, such as the type of animation (Entrance, Exit, Emphasis, or Motion Path), the sequence and timeline of the animation, and the name of the animated object. Clicking an animation's list arrow provides access to other custom options. Compare your screen to Figure F-9.

3. **Click ⬇ in the Animation group, click Fly In, then click the Duration up arrow in the Timing group until 1.00 appears**

   The Fly In entrance animation replaces the Random Bars entrance animation. A longer duration, or animation timing, slows down the animation.

4. **Click the Effect Options button in the Animation group, point to each option in the Direction and Sequence sections of the gallery and watch the Live Preview of the animation, then click By Elements in Series in the Sequence section**

   Each data series marker, by series, flies in from the left of the slide beginning with the Standard Rail data series. There are now 13 animation tags, one for the chart background and one for each data series marker.

5. **Click the Expand contents arrow ⬇ in the Animation Pane, click the first animation tag 1 on the slide, click Fade in the Animation group, then click the Duration up arrow until 1.50 appears**

   The Fade animation is now applied to the chart background. Notice the timeline icon for the chart background animation is wider to account for the longer duration.

6. **Click the Play button in the Animation Pane, then watch all the animations**

   The chart background fades into view, then data series markers fly in from the left one after another. Notice the advancing timeline (vertical blue line) as it moves over each animation in the Animation Pane.

7. **Click the Hide contents arrow ⬆ in the Animation Pane, click the Delay up arrow until .50 appears, then click the Play button in the Animation Pane**

   A half second delay is applied between each animation. Watch closely at how the changed settings affect the progression of the animated data series markers.

8. **Click the Start list arrow in the Timing group, click After Previous, click the Trigger button in the Advanced Animation group, point to On Click of, then click Title 1**

   Now when Slide 11 appears in Slide Show view, you can click the slide title to play the chart animations. The animation tags combine into one lightning bolt tag indicating the animation has a trigger.

9. **Click the Slide Show button ⬛ on the status bar, click the slide title, watch the animation, press [Esc], close the Animation Pane, then save the presentation**

   Compare your screen to Figure F-10.

**FIGURE F-9:** Screen showing added animation effect

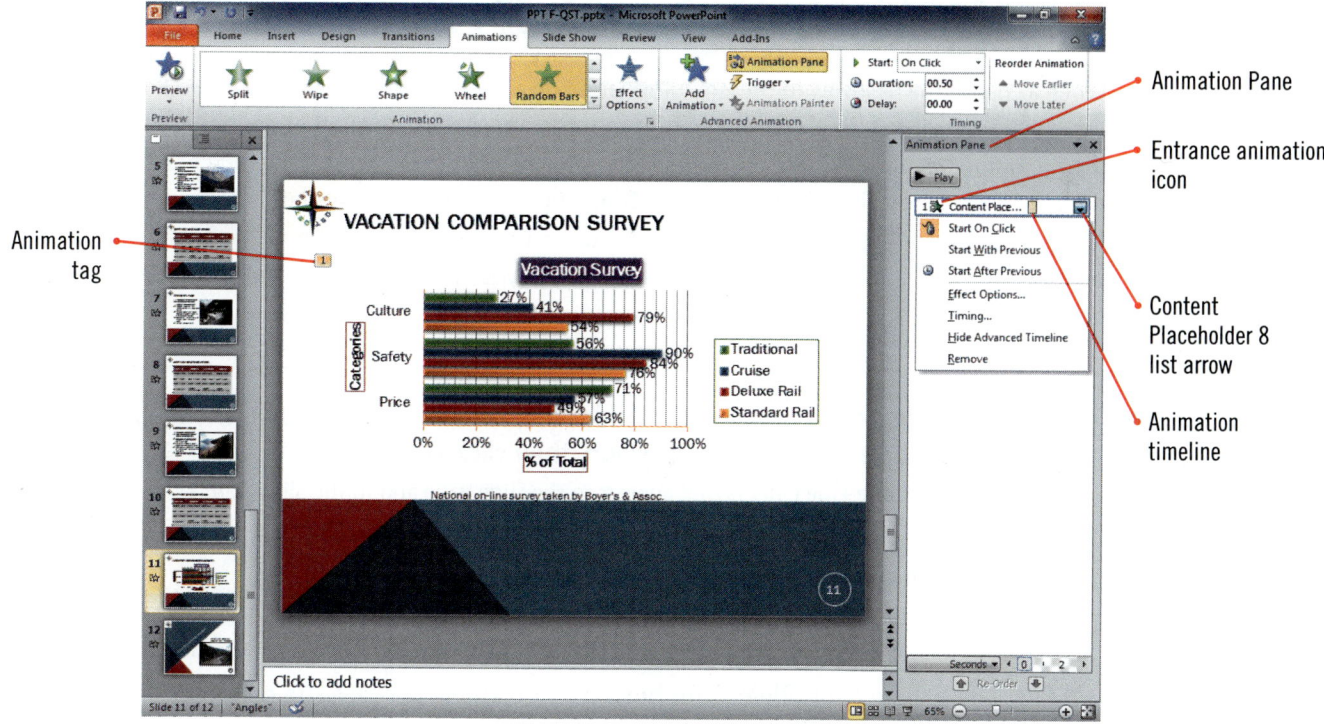

Animation tag

Animation Pane

Entrance animation icon

Content Placeholder 8 list arrow

Animation timeline

**FIGURE F-10:** Finished chart

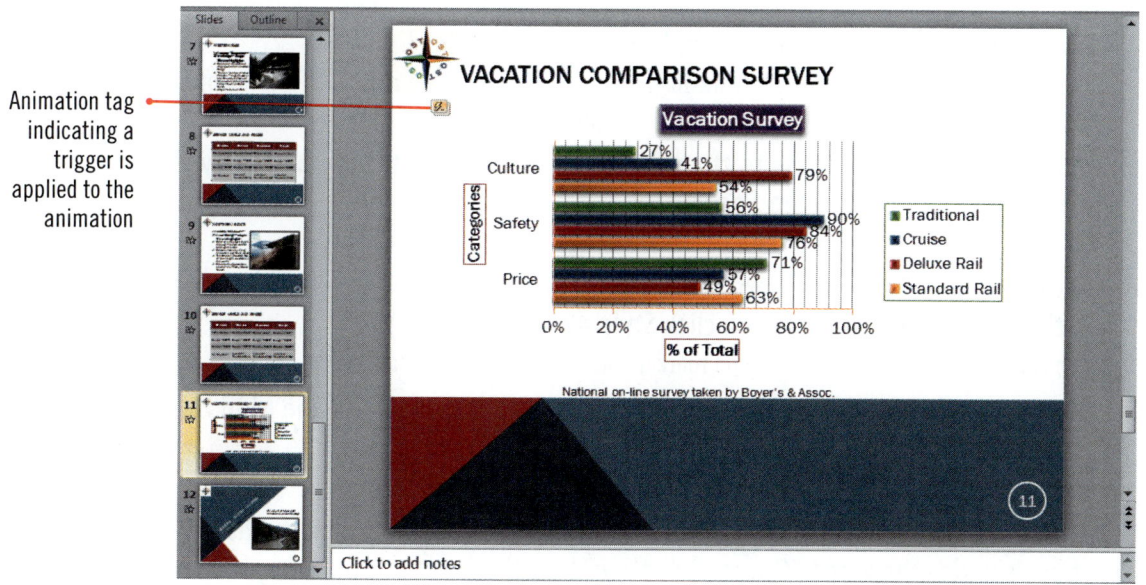

Animation tag indicating a trigger is applied to the animation

## Adjusting screen resolution and improving performance

If your presentation runs too slow or shudders during a slide show, one possible solution is to adjust the resolution setting PowerPoint uses during a slide show. By default, the resolution used during a slide show is the resolution of the monitor displaying the show. To change the slide show resolution, click the Slide Show tab on the Ribbon, click the Resolution button in the Monitors group, then click a different resolution option. Lower resolutions provide faster speeds but poor picture quality, while higher resolutions provide slower speeds and better picture quality. Other ways to improve performance include reducing single letter and single word animations, reducing the size of animated pictures, and reducing the number of simultaneous animations. Objects that have gradient or transparent fills also slow performance.

# Embedding an Excel Chart

When a chart is the best way to present information on a slide, you can create one within PowerPoint or you can embed an existing Excel chart directly to the slide. When you use another program to create an object, the program, Excel in this case, is known as the **source program**. The object you create with the source program is saved to a file called the **source file**. When you embed a chart into a presentation, the presentation file in which the chart is embedded becomes the **destination file**. You want to include other supporting data from last year's sales numbers in your presentation, so you embed an Excel chart on a new slide.

## STEPS

**QUICK TIP**
You can also press [Ctrl][D] to duplicate a slide in the Slides tab.

1. **Click the Slide 12 thumbnail in the Slides tab, click the Home tab on the Ribbon, click the New Slide list arrow in the Slides group, then click Title Only**

   A new slide with the Title Only layout appears in the Slide pane and in the Slides tab.

2. **Click the slide title placeholder, type Quarterly Profit Figures, click the Insert tab on the Ribbon, then click the Object button in the Text group**

   The new slide title appears in capital letters because of the presentation theme. The Insert Object dialog box opens. Using this dialog box, you can create a new chart or locate an existing one to insert on a slide.

**QUICK TIP**
Another way to embed a chart is to open the chart in Excel, copy it, and then paste it into your slide.

3. **Click the Create from file option button, click Browse, locate the drive and folder where you store your Data Files, click the file PPT F-2.xlsx, click OK, then click OK in the Insert Object dialog box**

   The chart containing the quarterly profit figures appears and is embedded on the slide. You can open the chart and use the commands in Excel to make any changes to it.

4. **Double-click the chart to open it in Microsoft Office Excel**

   The chart appears inside an Excel worksheet on the slide. Excel commands and tabs appear on the Ribbon under the PowerPoint title bar as shown in Figure F-11.

5. **Click the Sheet 2 tab at the bottom of the Excel worksheet, click cell B5, type 17490.10, press [Enter], then click the Sheet 3 tab**

   The changed number is reflected for the Quarter 1 UK data series in the chart.

**QUICK TIP**
If the chart you want to embed is in another presentation, you can open both presentations and then copy and paste the chart from one presentation to the other.

6. **Click the chart, click the Chart Tools Design tab on the Ribbon, click the More button ⊡ in the Chart Styles group, then click Style 42 (bottom row)**

   The chart style changes with new data marker colors and a new plot area color.

7. **Right-click the Vertical (Value) Axis, click the Bold button B on the Mini toolbar, click the Horizontal (Category) Axis, then press [F4]**

   Both the value and category axes labels are bold and now easier to read.

8. **Click outside the chart to exit Excel, drag the chart's upper-left sizing handle until the chart is under the word "Quarterly", then drag the upper-right sizing handle up and to the right until the chart is directly under the slide title**

   Compare your screen to Figure F-12.

9. **Click a blank area of the slide, then save the presentation**

**FIGURE F-11:** Inserted Excel chart

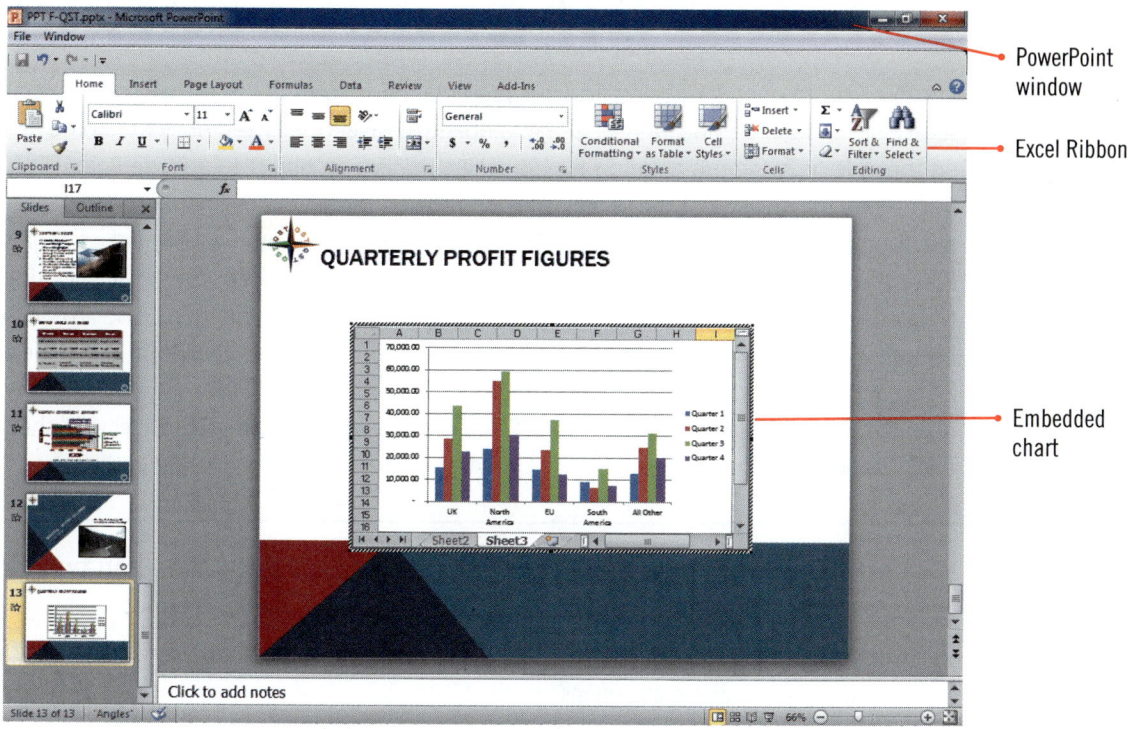

- PowerPoint window
- Excel Ribbon
- Embedded chart

**FIGURE F-12:** Formatted Excel chart

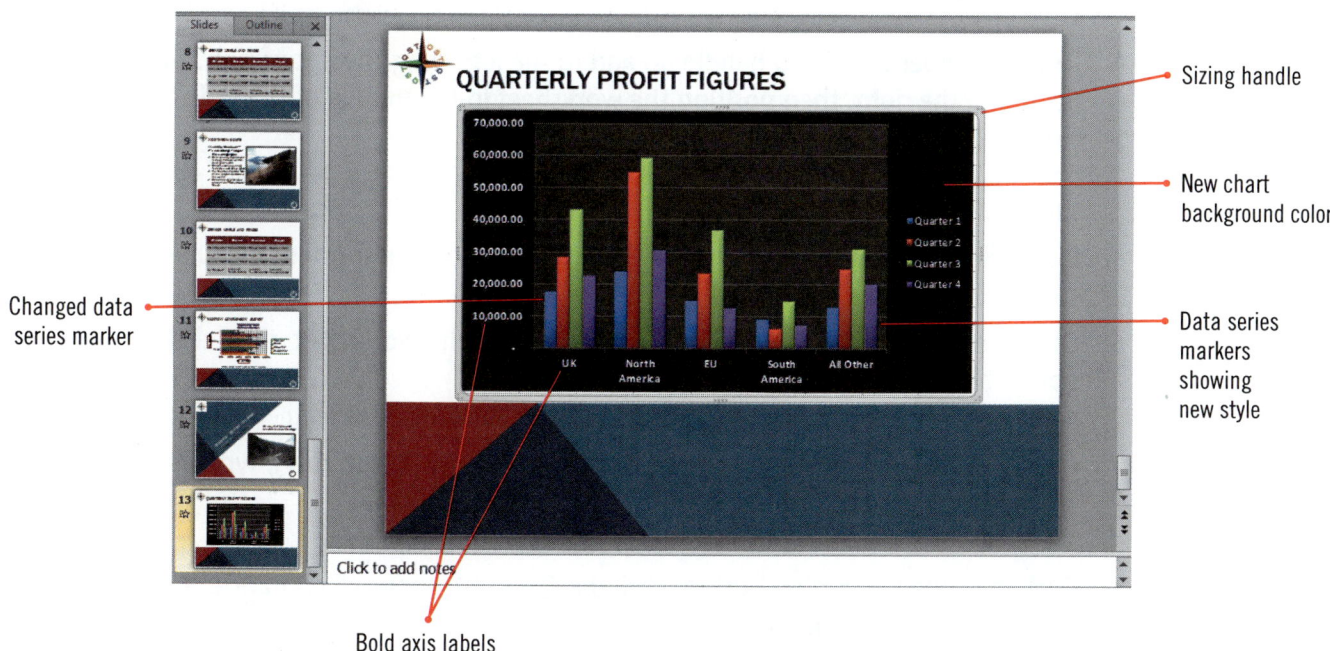

- Sizing handle
- New chart background color
- Data series markers showing new style
- Changed data series marker
- Bold axis labels

## Embedding a worksheet

You can embed all or part of an Excel worksheet in a PowerPoint slide. To embed an entire worksheet, go to the slide where you want to place the worksheet. Click the Insert tab on the Ribbon, then click the Object button in the Text group. The Insert Object dialog box opens. Click the Create from file option button, click Browse, locate and double-click the worksheet filename, then click OK. The worksheet is embedded in the slide. Double-click it to edit it using Excel commands as needed to work with the worksheet. To insert only a portion of a worksheet, open the Excel workbook and copy the cells you want to include in your presentation.

# Linking an Excel Worksheet

Another way to connect objects to your presentation is to establish a **link**, or connection, between the source file and the destination file. Unlike embedded objects, a linked object is stored in its source file, not on the slide or in the presentation file. So when you link an object to a PowerPoint slide, a representation (picture) of the object, not the object itself, appears on the slide. Any changes made to the source file using the source program of a linked object are automatically reflected in the linked representation in your PowerPoint presentation. Some of the objects that you can link to PowerPoint include bitmap images, Microsoft Excel worksheets, and PowerPoint slides from other presentations. Use linking when you want to be sure your presentation contains the latest information and when you want to include an object, such as an accounting spreadsheet, that may change over time. See Table F-1 for suggestions on when to embed an object and when to link an object.  You need to link and format an Excel worksheet to the presentation. The worksheet was created by the QST Accounting Department earlier in the year.

## STEPS

**QUICK TIP**

If you plan to do the steps in this lesson again, make a copy of the Excel file PPT F-3.xlsx to keep the original data intact.

1. **Click the Home tab on the Ribbon, click the New Slide button, then type QST Revenue**

   A new slide, Slide 14, is created and appears in the Slide pane and Slides tab.

2. **Click the Insert tab on the Ribbon, then click the Object button in the Text group**

   The Insert Object dialog box opens.

3. **Click the Create from file option button, click Browse, locate the file PPT F-3.xlsx in the drive and folder where you store your Data Files, click OK, click the Link check box, then click OK**

   The Excel worksheet appears on the slide. The worksheet would be easier to see if it were larger.

4. **Drag the upper-left sizing handle up and to the left, drag the upper-right sizing handle up and to the right, then position the worksheet in the middle of the slide as shown in Figure F-13**

   If the worksheet had a background fill color, it would help to emphasize the data and direct the audience's attention.

5. **Right-click the worksheet, then click Format Object on the shortcut menu**

   The Format Object dialog box opens.

6. **Drag the dialog box out of the way if it is blocking the worksheet, then click the Solid fill option button**

   A dark orange color is applied behind the worksheet. The color is too dark for the presentation.

7. **Click the Color list arrow , click Dark Green, Accent 4 (top row), type 40 in the Transparency text box, then click Line Color in the left pane**

   The transparency of the background color is at 40 percent and looks better.

8. **Click the Solid line option button, click the Color list arrow, click Orange, Accent 1, then click Line Style in the left pane**

   The worksheet appears with a new border color.

9. **Click the Width up arrow until 2pt appears, click Close, click a blank area of the slide, then save the presentation**

   The border is thicker and easier to see. Compare your screen to Figure F-14.

**FIGURE F-13:** Slide with linked Excel worksheet

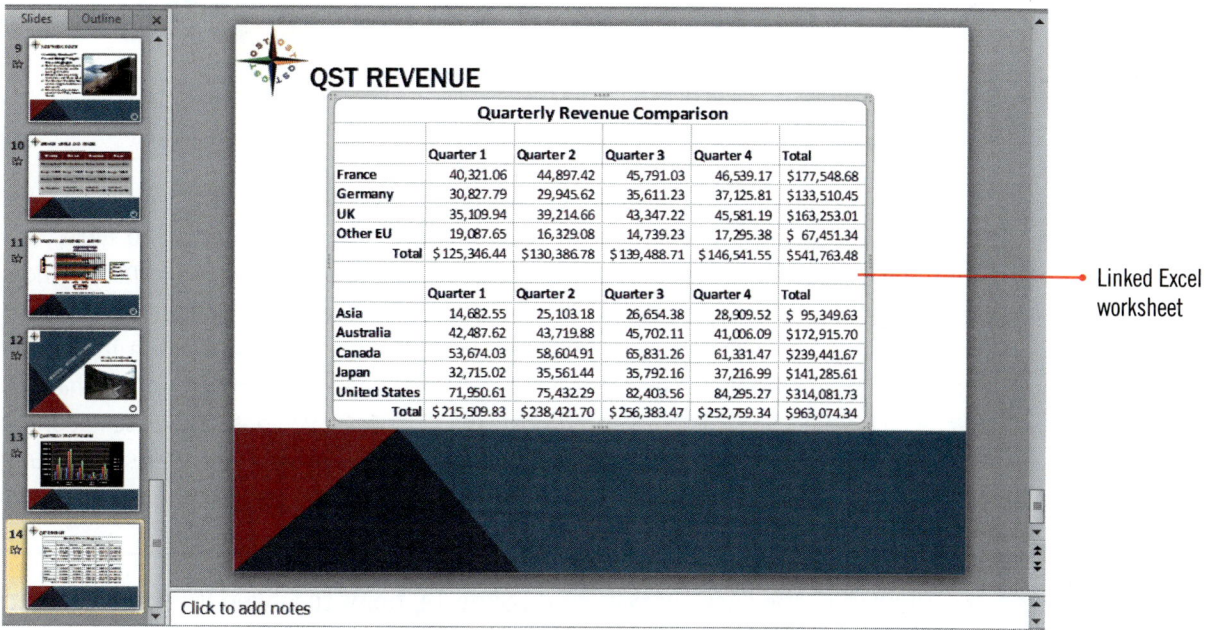

Linked Excel worksheet

**FIGURE F-14:** Formatted linked worksheet

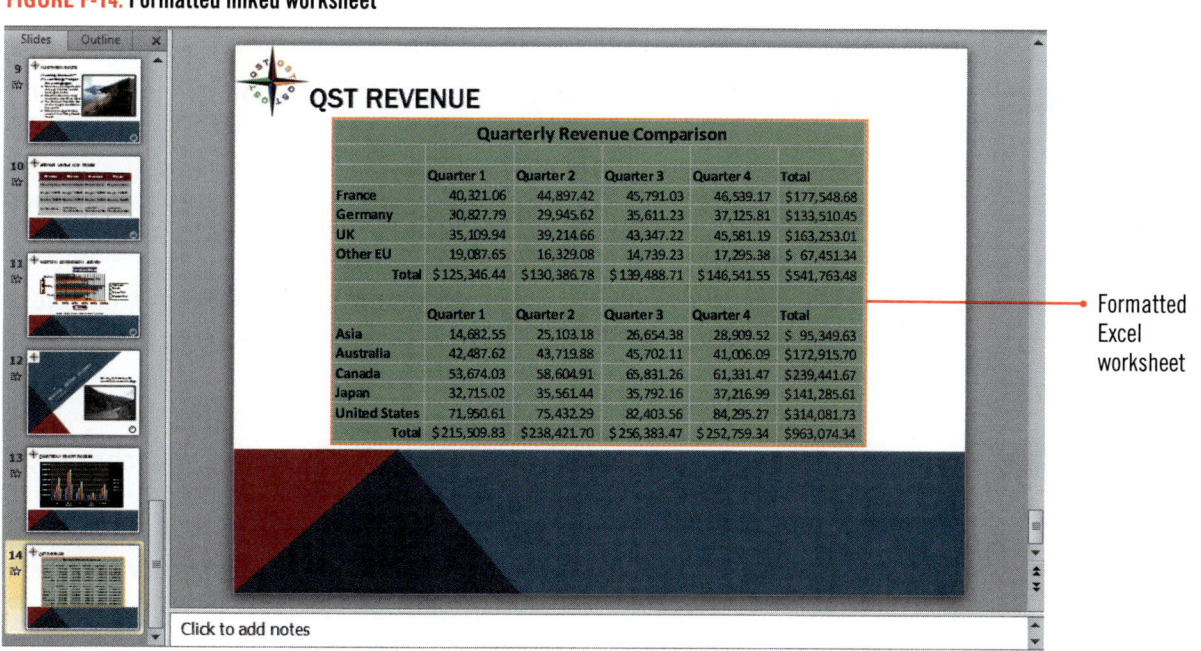

Formatted Excel worksheet

**TABLE F-1:** Embedding versus linking

| situation | action |
| --- | --- |
| When you are the only user of an object and you want the object to be a part of your presentation | Embed |
| When you want to access the object in its source program, even if the original file is not available | Embed |
| When you want to update the object manually while working in PowerPoint | Embed |
| When you always want the latest information in your object | Link |
| When the object's source file is shared on a network or when other users have access to the file and can change it | Link |
| When you want to keep your presentation file size small | Link |

# Updating a Linked Excel Worksheet

To edit or change the information in a linked object, you must open the object's source file in its source program. For example, you must open Microsoft Word to edit a linked Word table, or you must open Microsoft Excel to edit a linked Excel worksheet. You can open the source program by double-clicking the linked object in the PowerPoint slide, as you did with embedded objects, or by starting the source program directly using any method you prefer. When you work on a linked object in its source program, your PowerPoint presentation can be either open or closed. If data in the linked file has changed while the presentation is closed, you will be asked to update the slides when you open the presentation. You have just received an e-mail that some of the data in the Excel worksheet is incorrect, so you update the data in the linked worksheet.

## STEPS

> **QUICK TIP**
>
> You can also double-click the linked worksheet to open it in Excel.

1. **Right-click the Excel worksheet on Slide 14, point to Linked Worksheet Object, then click Edit**

   The worksheet PPT F-3.xlsx opens up in the Microsoft Excel window.

2. **Click cell D14, type 40826.76, click cell C5, type 26312.88, then press [Enter]**

   The Quarter 3 value for Japan and the Quarter 2 value for Germany change. All totals that include these values in the Total cells are updated accordingly. Compare your screen to Figure F-15.

> **QUICK TIP**
>
> To edit or open a linked object in your presentation, the object's source program and source file must be available on your computer or network.

3. **Click cell B4, press and hold [Shift], click cell E7, release [Shift], right-click in the selected cell area, then click the Accounting Number Format button $ ▾ on the Mini toolbar**

   All of the selected cells now have the accounting format and display the dollar symbol.

4. **Click cell B11, drag to cell E15, then press [F4]**

   The same accounting number format is applied to these cells.

5. **Click cell F8, press [Ctrl], click cell F16, click the Bold button B in the Font group, click the Bottom Border list arrow ▦ ▾ in the Font group, click Thick Box Border, then click a blank cell**

   The bold font attribute and a black border is added to cells F8 and F16 to highlight the overall totals.

> **QUICK TIP**
>
> If your presentation is closed when you update a linked object, a security dialog box opens the next time you open your presentation. Click Update Links in the dialog box to update the linked object.

6. **Click the Excel window Close button ✕, click Save to save your changes, then click a blank area of the slide**

   The Excel window closes. The Excel worksheet in the PPT F-QST.pptx presentation file is now updated with the new data and shows the formatting changes you made. PowerPoint automatically makes all of the changes to the linked object. Compare your screen to Figure F-16.

7. **Check the spelling, add your name as the footer to the handouts, save the presentation, then submit your presentation to your instructor**

   If your instructor requires you to print your presentation, then use the print layout setting 6 Slides Horizontal.

8. **Close the presentation, then exit PowerPoint**

**FIGURE F-15:** Modified Excel worksheet

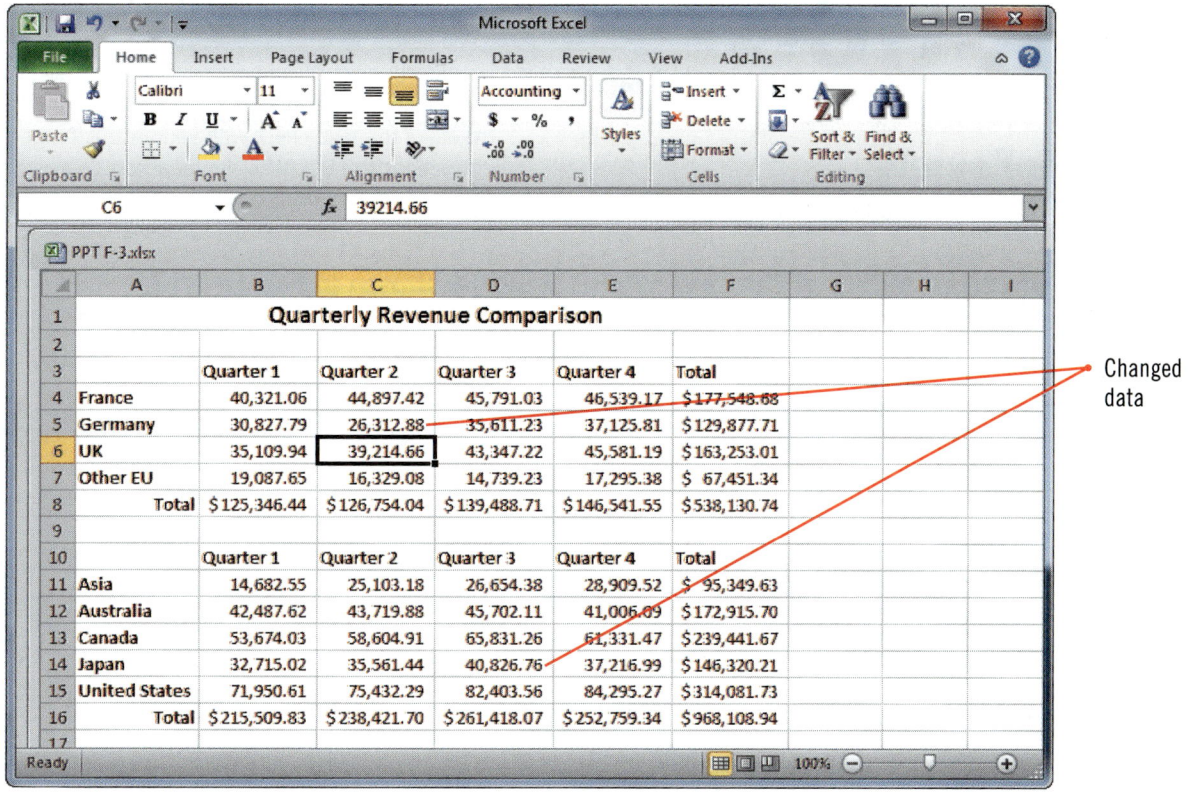

Changed data

**FIGURE F-16:** Slide with updated worksheet

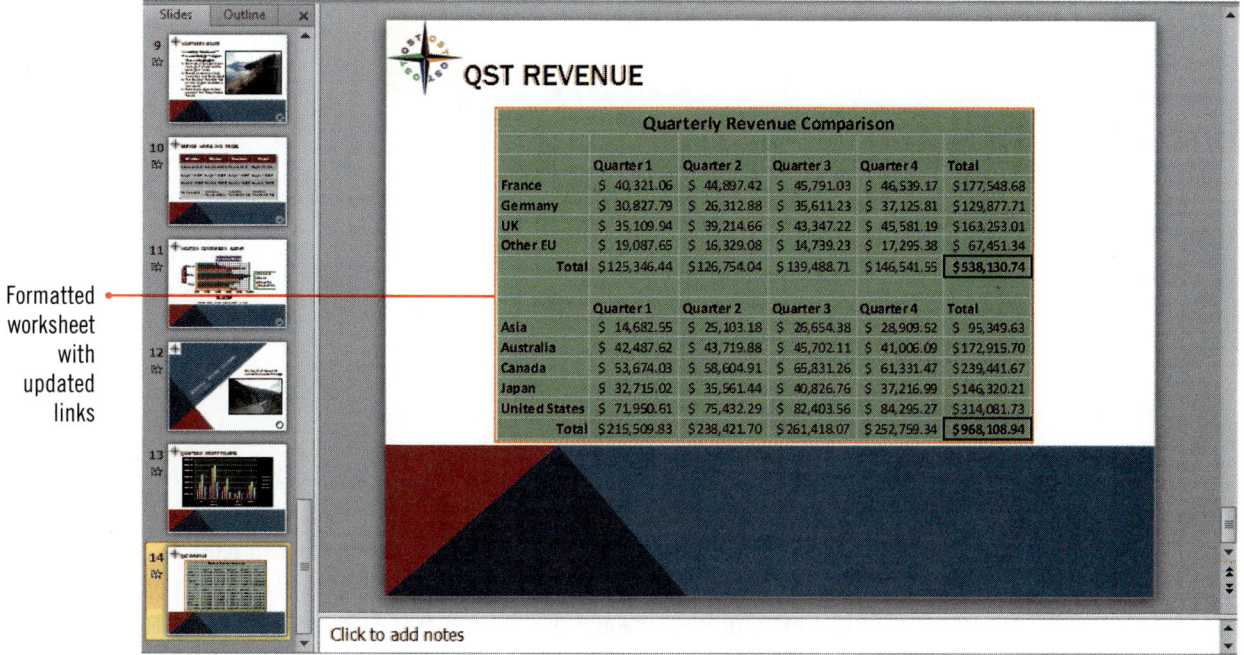

Formatted worksheet with updated links

## Editing links

Once you link an object to your presentation, you have the ability to edit its link. Using the Links dialog box, you can update a link, open or change a linked object's source file, break a link, and determine if a linked object is updated manually or automatically. The Links dialog box is the only place where you can change a linked object's source file, break a link, and change the link updating method. To open the Links dialog box, click the File tab on the Ribbon, then click Edit Links to Files button under Related Documents in the right pane.

# Practice

For current SAM information, including versions and content details, visit SAM Central (http://www.cengage.com/samcentral). If you have a SAM user profile, you may have access to hands-on instruction, practice, and assessment of the skills covered in this unit. Since various versions of SAM are supported throughout the life of this text, check with your instructor for the correct instructions and URL/Web site for accessing assignments.

## Concepts Review

**Label each of the elements of the PowerPoint window shown in Figure F-17.**

FIGURE F-17

![PowerPoint window screenshot labeled 1 through 8 showing the Animations ribbon, a slide with a "VACATION COMPARISON SURVEY" bar chart, and the Animation Pane]

**Match each of the terms with the statement that describes its function.**

9. **Trend**

10. **Major gridlines**

11. **Error bars**

12. **Source file**

13. **Template**

a. Identifies potential data mistakes relative to each data marker in a data series

b. A chart formatting and layout that is saved so you can reuse it

c. The file that contains the embedded object you insert into a PowerPoint file

d. A main unit on the axis of a chart that is usually identified by a tick mark

e. A graphical representation of an upward or downward tendency in a data series

**Select the best answer from the list of choices.**

14. A(n) _____ chart displays data from one data series in proportion to the sum of all of the data series.
    - **a.** pie
    - **b.** doughnut
    - **c.** surface
    - **d.** area

15. What helps make the data easier to read in the chart and extends from the horizontal or vertical axes across the plot area?
    - **a.** Data markers
    - **b.** Gridlines
    - **c.** A range of data
    - **d.** Tick marks

16. Which animation method would you use to display each data series marker independently with the same color?
    - **a.** By series
    - **b.** Individually by series
    - **c.** Individually by category
    - **d.** By category

17. Which of the statements below is *not true* about working with charts in PowerPoint?
    - **a.** Microsoft Graph is used to create a chart if Excel is not available.
    - **b.** A linked chart is saved in the presentation.
    - **c.** Document themes and effects are consistent between PowerPoint and Excel.
    - **d.** An embedded chart's data is stored in an Excel worksheet.

18. Small lines that intersect an axis and identify categories are called _____.
    - **a.** category markers
    - **b.** tick marks
    - **c.** plot layout lines
    - **d.** chart wedges

19. You use a _____ program to create an object that you insert into PowerPoint.
    - **a.** support
    - **b.** destination
    - **c.** linked
    - **d.** source

20. To apply the styles of a presentation to an object, you would use the _____ paste method.
    - **a.** use destination styles
    - **b.** keep source formatting
    - **c.** keep text only
    - **d.** embed

## Skills Review

1. **Change chart design and style.**
   a. Start PowerPoint, open the presentation PPT F-4.pptx, then save it as **PPT F-Lucio Bros** to the drive and folder where you store your Data Files.
   b. Click Slide 3 in the Slides pane, then select the chart.
   c. Open the Chart Tools Design tab, then apply Layout 7 from the Chart Layouts group.
   d. Change the label on the Vertical (Value) Axis to **Millions**, and then change the Horizontal (Category) Axis label to **Divisions**.
   e. Apply Style 28 from the Chart Styles group.
   f. Change the chart type to Clustered Cylinder. (*Hint*: A cylinder is a type of column chart.)

2. **Customize a chart layout.**
   a. Open the Chart Tools Layout tab, then change the horizontal gridlines to major gridlines and the vertical gridlines to major gridlines.
   b. Click the Chart Floor button in the Background group, click More Floor Options, click the Solid fill option button, click the Color list arrow, click Ice Blue, Text 2, then click Close.

# Skills Review (continued)

    **c.** Right-click the value axis label, click the Shape Outline button arrow on the Mini toolbar, then click White, Text 1.

    **d.** Select the category axis title, then press [F4].

    **e.** Click a blank area of the chart, then save your changes.

**3. Format chart elements.**

    **a.** Open the Chart Tools Layout tab, click the Chart Area list arrow in the Current Selection group, then click Series "2nd Qtr."

    **b.** Click the Format Selection button in the Current Selection group, then drag the Gap Width slider to the left to about 150%.

    **c.** Click Fill in the left pane, then change the fill to a gradient fill, click the Direction list arrow, then click Linear Down.

    **d.** Click 3-D Format in the left pane, click the Material list arrow, click Dark Edge, then click Close.

    **e.** Right-click the value axis, then click Format Axis.

    **f.** Under Axis Options click the Major unit Fixed option button, then type **15** in the text box.

    **g.** Click the Major tick mark type list arrow, click Cross, click Close, then save your changes.

**4. Animate a chart.**

    **a.** Select the Animations tab, then apply the Float In Entrance animation to the chart.

    **b.** Click the Effect Options button, then change the animation to By Element in Category.

    **c.** Click the Animation Pane button, click the Object 4 list arrow in the Animation Pane, click Effect Options, then click the Chart Animation tab.

    **d.** Click the check box to not draw the chart background, then click OK.

    **e.** Change the duration to 1.50 and the delay to .75 for all the animations.

    **f.** Close the Animation Pane, then save your changes.

**5. Embed an Excel chart.**

    **a.** Select Slide 4, then click the Insert tab.

    **b.** Click the Object button in the Text group, click the Create from file option button, click Browse, locate and open the file PPT F-5.xlsx from the drive and folder where you store your Data Files, then click OK.

    **c.** Double-click the chart, then drag the right-middle sizing handle so the extra column next to the legend is hidden from view.

    **d.** Click the Chart Tools Design tab, then change the chart style to Style 40.

    **e.** Change the horizontal gridlines to display only major gridlines.

    **f.** Right-click the legend, click the Shape Outline list arrow on the Mini toolbar, click Automatic, then click a blank area of the slide.

    **g.** Resize the chart so it fills most of the slide, then save your changes.

**6. Link an Excel worksheet.**

    **a.** Add a new slide after the current slide with the Title Only layout.

    **b.** Type **Lucio Bros. Publishing**, click the Insert tab, then click the Object button in the Text group.

    **c.** Click the Create from file option button, locate the file PPT F-6.xlsx in the drive and folder where you store your Data Files, then link it to the slide.

    **d.** Resize the worksheet object by dragging its sizing handles.

    **e.** Right-click the worksheet, click Format Object, click the Solid fill option button, click the Color list arrow, then click Orange, Accent 3.

    **f.** Change the transparency to 25%, click Close, then save your changes.

## Skills Review (continued)

**7. Update a linked Excel worksheet.**

a. Double-click the worksheet.

b. Select cells B5 to F9, click the Accounting Number Format list arrow in the Number group, then click Euro.

c. Click cell F9, then click the Bold button in the Font group.

d. Click cell D5, type **72492.38**, click cell E7, then type **87253.11**.

e. Close the Excel window, then click Save to save your changes. The changes appear in the linked worksheet. Figure F-18 shows the completed presentation.

f. Add your name to the handout footer, save your work, submit your presentation to your instructor, close the presentation, and exit PowerPoint.

# Independent Challenge 1

You work for Madison & Sons Inc., a business consulting company that helps businesses organize or restructure themselves to be more efficient and profitable. You are one of four consultants who work directly with clients. To prepare for an upcoming meeting with executives at a local Internet communications company, you create a brief presentation outlining typical investigative and reporting techniques, past results versus the competition, and the company's business philosophy. Use PowerPoint to customize a chart on Slide 5 of the presentation.

a. Start PowerPoint, open the presentation PPT F-7.pptx from the drive and folder where you store your Data Files, then save it as **PPT F-Madison**.

b. Select the chart on Slide 5, then apply Layout 3 from the Chart Layouts gallery.

c. Apply Style 29 from the Chart Styles gallery, then type **AMPI Rating Comparison** in the chart title text box.

d. Change the chart type to Clustered Bar, then add minor vertical gridlines to the chart.

e. Right-click the value axis, click Format Axis, click Number in the left pane, click Number in the Category list, type **1** in the Decimal Places text box, then click Close.

f. Click the Data Labels button, then show data labels using the Outside End option.

### Advanced Challenge Exercise

■ Right-click the value axis, click Format Axis, click the Major unit Fixed option button, then type **0.5**.

■ Click the Minor unit Fixed option button, type **0.1**, then click Close

■ Right-click the category axis, click Format Axis, click Alignment in the left pane, type **–25** in the Custom angle text box, then click Close.

g. Change the data labels to the Inside End option, then check the spelling in the presentation.

h. Add your name as a footer to the slides and handouts, then view the presentation in Reading View.

i. Save the presentation, submit your presentation to your instructor, close the presentation, then exit PowerPoint.

# Independent Challenge 2

One of your responsibilities working in the Kansas State Schools system is to provide program performance data for educational programs designed for disabled children in the state. You need to develop and give a presentation describing the program's results at a national education forum held this year in Denver, Colorado. You have been working on the presentation, and now you need to use PowerPoint to put the finishing touches on a chart.

a. Start PowerPoint, open the presentation PPT F-8.pptx from the drive and folder where you store your Data Files, then save it as **PPT F-Kansas**.

b. Select Slide 7, select the chart, then change the chart style to Style 31.

c. Click the Chart Tools Layout tab click the 3-D Rotation button, then in the Rotation section click the X up arrow once.

d. Open the Chart Tools Format tab, select the Math data series, then change the shape fill to the gradient From Center.

e. Change the Reading data series to the Cork texture shape fill, click the Chart Tools Design tab, then change the chart layout to Layout 7.

f. Type **APCI Score** in the vertical axis label, then type **Grade Level** in the horizontal axis label.

g. Apply the Wipe Entrance animation to the chart, then change the Effect options to By Category.

h. Check the spelling in the presentation, add your name as a footer to the slides and handouts, then save the presentation.

i. View the presentation in Slide Show view, submit your presentation to your instructor, close the presentation, then exit PowerPoint.

# Independent Challenge 3

Hanover Mark Industries is a large company that develops and produces medical equipment and technical machines for operating and emergency rooms throughout the United States. You are one of the client representatives in the company, and one of your assignments is to prepare a presentation for the division management meetings on the profitability and efficiency of each division in the company. Use PowerPoint to develop the presentation.

a. Open the file PPT F-9.pptx from the drive and folder where you store your Data Files, then save it as **PPT F-Hanover**.

b. Apply the Clarity theme, then add at least two graphics to the presentation.

c. Add a new slide after the title slide titled **Company Divisions**, then create a SmartArt graphic that identifies the company's seven divisions: Administration, Accounting, Sales and Marketing, Research and Development, Product Testing, Product Development, and Manufacturing.

d. Format the new SmartArt graphic using SmartArt Styles and colors.

e. Select the Division Performance slide, then insert the Excel file PPT F-10.xlsx from the drive and folder where you store your Data Files.

f. Drag the corner sizing handles of the chart so it covers most of the slide, then double-click the chart.

**Advanced Challenge Exercise**

- Click the Chart Tools Layout tab, click the Trendline button in the Analysis group, click Linear Trendline, click Sales, then click OK.
- Right-click the value axis, then click Format Axis.
- Click the Minor tick mark type list arrow, then click Outside, then click Close.

g. Apply the Style 42 chart style to the chart, right-click the category axis, click Format Axis, click the Axis labels list arrow, click Low, then click Close.

h. Select the Division Budgets slide, then link the Excel file PPT F-11.xlsx from the drive and folder where you store your Data Files.

i. Open the linked worksheet in Excel, select cells B5 through F12, click the Accounting Number Format button in the Number group, save the changes to the worksheet, then close Excel.

# Independent Challenge 3 (continued)

**j.** Right-click the linked chart, click Format Object, click the Solid fill option button, change the fill color to Red, Text 2 at 25% transparency.

**k.** Resize the worksheet to fill the slide, add your name as a footer to the slides and handouts, check the spelling, then view your presentation in Slide Show view.

**l.** Submit your presentation to your instructor, close the presentation and exit PowerPoint.

# Real Life Independent Challenge

You are on staff at your college newspaper. One of your jobs is to review computer games and post a presentation on the paper's Web site. The presentation identifies the top computer games based on student testing and other reviews. Use PowerPoint to create a presentation that includes research and your own information. Use the basic presentation provided as a basis to develop this presentation.

As you create this presentation, follow these guidelines:

- Include three computer games in your presentation.
- Each game has at least one defined mission or task.
- Consumer satisfaction of each game is identified on a scale of 1.0 to 10.0.
- There are three categories of games: Adventure, Action, and Strategy.
- Presentation should include at least eight slides, including the title slide.

If you have access to the Web, you can research the following topics to help you develop information for your presentation:

- Consumer or industry reviews of computer games
- Computer game descriptions and pricing

**a.** Connect to the Internet, then use a search engine to locate Web sites that have information on PC computer games. Review at least two Web sites that contain information about computer games. Print the home pages of the Web sites you use to gather data for your presentation.

**b.** Open the presentation PPT F-12.pptx from the drive and folder where you store your Data Files, then save it as **PPT F-Review**.

**c.** Add your name as the footer on all slides and handouts.

**d.** (Before you complete this step make a copy of the Data File PPT F-13.xlsx.) Link the Excel chart PPT F-13.xlsx from the drive and folder where you store your Data Files on the Game Reviews slide.

**e.** Resize the chart on the slide, then open the linked chart in Excel.

**f.** Click the Sheet 1 tab at the bottom of the Excel window, provide a name for each game, click the Sheet 2 tab, then save your changes.

**g.** Right-click the chart legend, click Delete on the shortcut menu, click the Page Layout tab, click the Colors button in the Themes group, then click Austin.

**h.** Save your changes, then exit Excel.

**i.** Create at least one SmartArt diagram that briefly explains the specifications of one of the games.

**j.** Create a table that lists the price of each game.

**k.** Enhance the presentation with clip art or other graphics, an appropriate design theme, and other items that improve the look of the presentation.

**l.** Modify the Slide Master as necessary.

**m.** Check the spelling in the presentation, save the presentation, then view the presentation in Slide Show view.

**n.** Add your name as a footer to the slides and handouts, submit your presentation to your instructor, close the presentation, then exit PowerPoint.

# Visual Workshop

Create a slide that looks like the example in Figure F-19. Start a new presentation, then insert the Excel worksheet PPT F-14.xlsx from the drive and folder where you store your Data Files. (*Hint*: The worksheet is formatted with a 60% transparent dark blue fill and a gold 3 point border.) Save the presentation as **PPT F-Wise Inc**. Add your name as a footer to the slides, then submit your presentation to your instructor.

**FIGURE F-19**

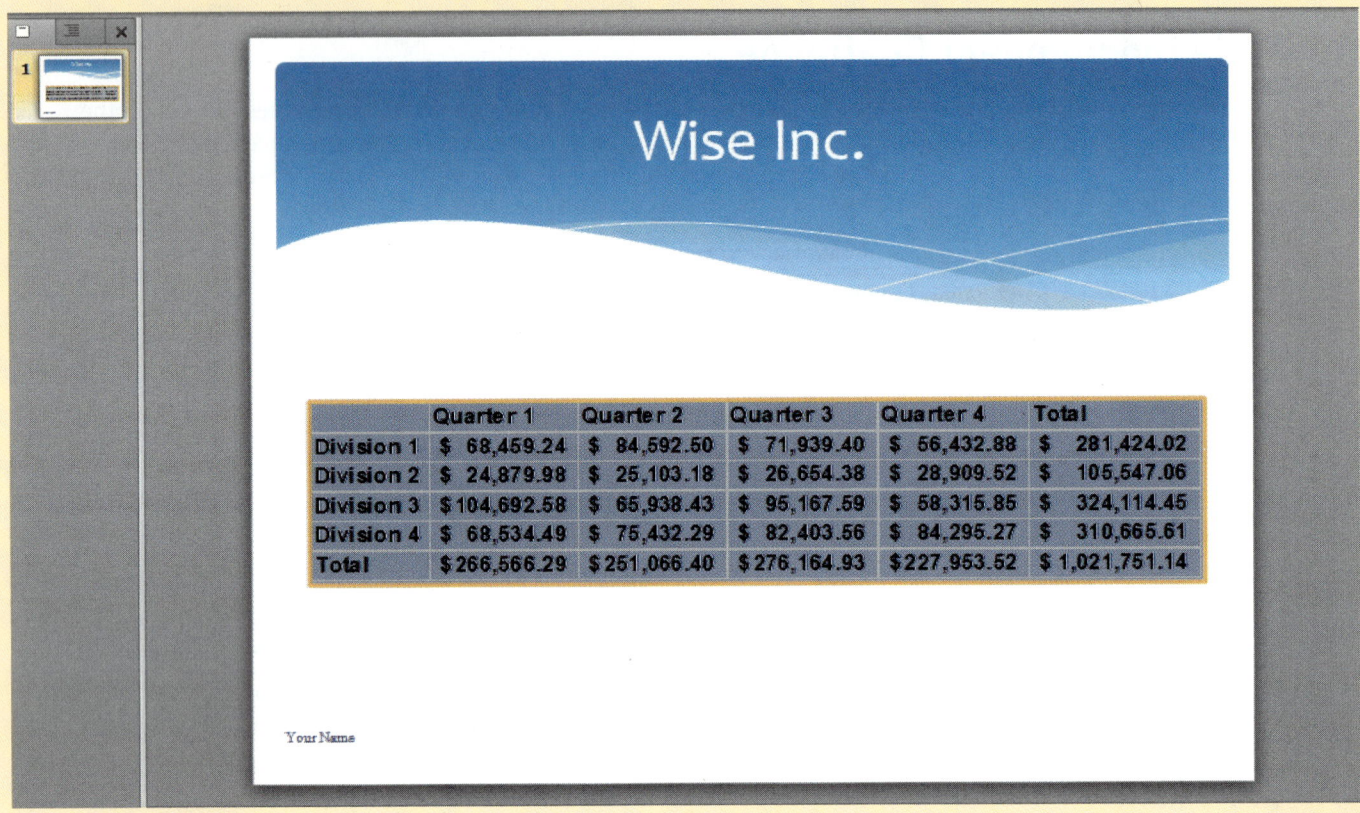

# Inserting Graphics, Media, and Objects

PowerPoint provides you with many different types of illustrations to improve your presentation. From customized tables and professional-looking graphics to videos and sounds, you have a wide range of options when it comes to developing your presentation. You also have other advanced tools, such as macros, hyperlinks, and action buttons that help correlate, simplify, and assimilate information. In this unit, you work on a short presentation that describes other tour opportunities that you link to the primary Train Tour presentation you have been working on for Quest Specialty Travel. You use the advanced features in PowerPoint to customize a table and a SmartArt graphic, then you insert a video and sound that complements the information. Finally, you use a macro to insert some pictures, create action buttons, and link one presentation to another one.

## OBJECTIVES

Create custom tables

Design a SmartArt graphic

Format a SmartArt graphic

Insert clip art video

Insert a sound

Use macros

Add action buttons

Insert a hyperlink

# Creating Custom Tables

A table is a great way to display and organize related information. In PowerPoint, you have the ability to create dynamic-looking tables. Tables you create in PowerPoint automatically display the style as determined by the theme assigned to the slide, including color combinations and shading, line styles and colors, and other attributes. It is easy to customize the layout of a table or change how data is organized. You can delete and insert rows or columns, merge two or more cells together, or split one cell into more cells. You open a short presentation on Canadian Train Add-On Tours that you have been working on and finish customizing a table.

## STEPS

**QUICK TIP**

As a rule, you should not enable macros from unfamiliar sources or those you do not trust because they could contain viruses.

1. **Start PowerPoint, open the presentation PPT G-1.pptm from the drive and folder where you store your Data Files, then click the Enable Content button in the Security Warning banner**

   Although this presentation looks similar to other presentations it has the file extension .pptm instead of .pptx. The .pptm file extension identifies the PowerPoint file as having macros attached to it. A **macro** is a set of actions that you use to automate tasks. You enabled the macros attached to this presentation.

2. **Save the presentation as PPT G-QST Link, click OK in the privacy warning message box, then click the Slide 2 thumbnail in the Slides tab**

   The Security Warning banner closes, and Slide 2 appears in the Slide pane.

3. **Click the table on Slide 2, click the Table Tools Design tab on the Ribbon, click the Pen Style button in the Draw Borders group, then click the dash-dot-dot style (5th style)**

   The pointer changes to ⌀, which indicates that you are in drawing mode.

4. **Click the white vertical column line that divides the Pricing and Includes columns in the first row in table, then click the vertical column line for each row in that column to the bottom of the table**

   Compare your screen to Figure G-1.

**QUICK TIP**

Press [Esc] to end drawing mode.

5. **Click the Draw Table button in the Draw Borders group, click the Table Tools Layout tab on the Ribbon, click the Walking Bicycle cell, then click the Split Cells button in the Merge group**

   Clicking the Draw Table button turns the drawing mode off and changes the pointer back to ⌀. Clicking the Split Cells button opens the Split Cells dialog box. The default table is 2 columns and 1 row, and the Number of columns text box is selected.

6. **Type 1 in the Number of columns text box, click the Number of rows up arrow once, then click OK**

   You split the cell to create a new row in that cell.

**QUICK TIP**

To change the text direction in a text box or a table, select the text, click the Text Direction button in the Paragraph group, then click the appropriate option.

7. **Double-click to select the word Bicycle, click the Home tab on the Ribbon, click the Cut button ✄ in the Clipboard group, press [Backspace], click the new row, click the Paste list arrow in the Clipboard group, then click the Keep Source Formatting button 🗒**

   The words "Walking" and "Bicycle" are now in two separate rows within the Transportation column. See Table G-1 for more information on Paste button options.

8. **Repeat Steps 5–7 to split the Bicycle pricing data in the Pricing column into two rows as shown in Figure G-2**

   Now the Bicycle information is separate from the Walking information.

9. **Click outside the table, save your presentation, then click OK in the privacy warning message box**

**FIGURE G-1:** Table with new column line style

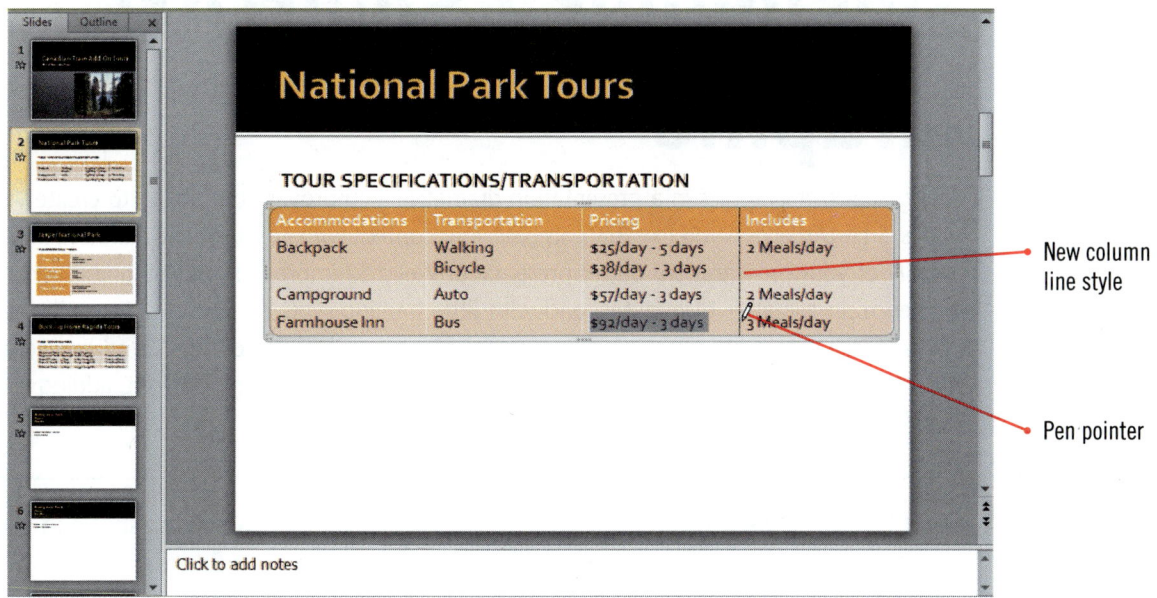

New column line style

Pen pointer

**FIGURE G-2:** New row with data

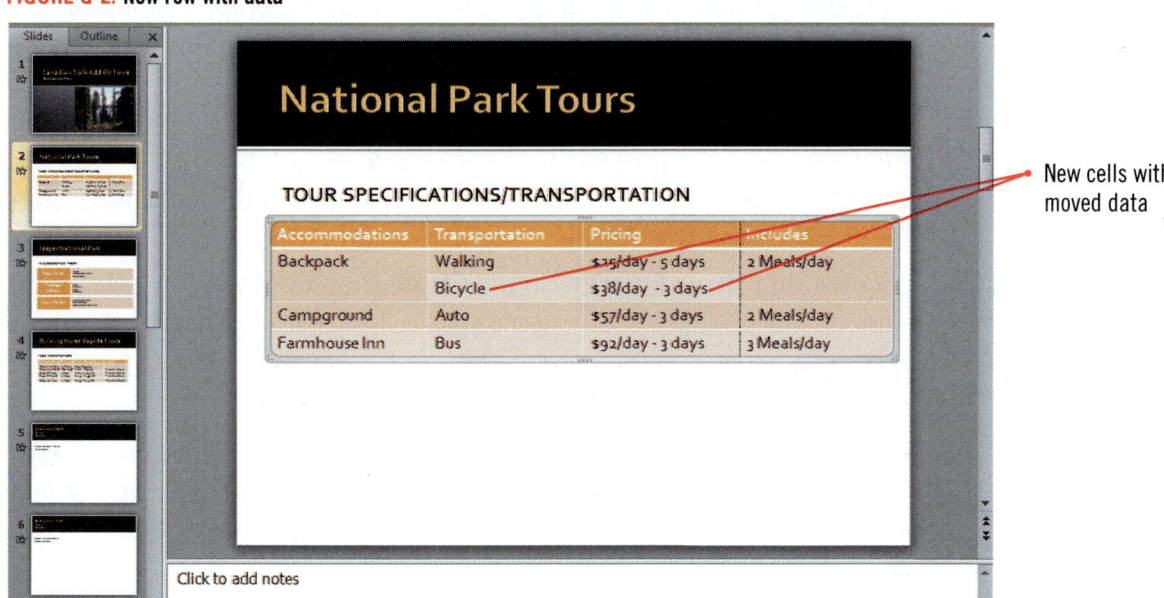

New cells with moved data

**TABLE G-1:** Understanding common Paste button options

| symbol | button name | result |
| --- | --- | --- |
| | **Keep Source Formatting** | Uses the formatting characteristics from the object's source file |
| | **Use Destination Styles** | Uses the current styles of the presentation |
| | **Embed** | Inserts the object as an embedded object |
| | **Picture** | Inserts the object as a picture |
| | **Keep Text Only** | Inserts the object as text only with no formatting |
| | **Use Destination Theme** | Uses the current theme of the presentation |

# Designing a SmartArt Graphic

Using SmartArt graphics in a presentation dramatically improves your ability to create vibrant content on slides. SmartArt allows you to easily combine your content with an illustrative diagram, improving the overall quality of your presentation. Better presentations lead to improved understanding and retention by your audience. In a matter of minutes, and with little training, you can create a SmartArt graphic using slide content that would otherwise have been placed in a simple bulleted list. You continue working on the Canadian Train Add-On tours presentation by changing the graphic layout, adding a shape and text to the SmartArt graphic, and then changing its color and style.

## STEPS

1. **Click the Slide 3 thumbnail in the Slides tab, click the Tour Sites shape in the SmartArt graphic, then click the SmartArt Tools Design tab on the Ribbon**

   The Tour Sites shape is selected and displays sizing handles and a rotate handle. Each shape in the SmartArt graphic is separate and distinct from the other shapes and can be individually edited, formatted, or moved within the boundaries of the SmartArt graphic.

2. **If necessary, click the Text Pane button in the Create Graphic group to open the Text pane, click the Add Bullet button in the Create Graphic group, then type Kamloops in the Text pane**

   A new bullet appears in the Text pane and in the upper-right shape of the graphic. Compare your screen with Figure G-3.

3. **Click the More button ⊟ in the Layouts group, then click Horizontal Picture List (3rd row)**

   The SmartArt graphic layout changes.

4. **Click the Add Shape list arrow in the Create Graphic group, then click Add Shape After**

   A new shape in the same style appears and a new bullet appears in the Text pane.

5. **Type Upgrades, press [Enter], press [Tab], type Add trip to Victoria BC, press [Enter], type Shopping in Banff, press [Enter], then type Personal guide**

6. **Click the More button ⊟ in the SmartArt Styles group, click Subtle Effect in the Best Match section, then click the Change Colors button in the SmartArt Styles group**

   A gallery of color themes appears showing the current theme applied to the graphic in the Accent 1 section.

7. **Click Colorful - Accent Colors in the Colorful section**

   Each shape now has its own color.

8. **Click the Text Pane button in the Create Graphic group, then click the Right to Left button in the Create Graphic group**

   The graphic flips and appears as a mirror image. You prefer the original view of the graphic.

9. **Click the Right to Left button, click a blank area of the slide, save your changes, then click OK in the privacy warning message box**

   Compare your screen to Figure G-4.

**QUICK TIP**
While the Text pane is open, use the Promote and Demote buttons to increase or decrease the level of the bullet or shape in the graphic.

**FIGURE G-3:** SmartArt graphic with added text

Text pane

Added text

**FIGURE G-4:** SmartArt graphic with new design

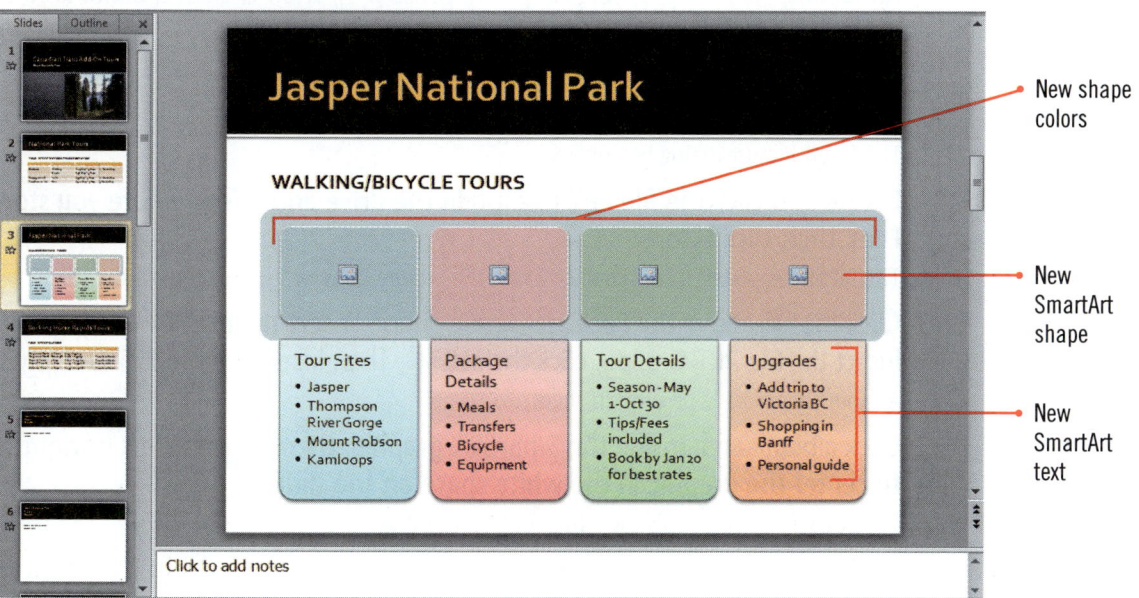

New shape colors

New SmartArt shape

New SmartArt text

## Creating mathematical equations

You can insert or create mathematical equations using the Equation button in the Symbols group on the Insert tab. Click the Equation button list arrow to access nine common equations, which include the area of a circle, the Pythagorean theorem (my personal favorite), and the quadratic formula. To create your own equations click the Equation button to open the Equation Tools Design tab. To help you create equations, you have access to eight types of symbols including basic math, geometry, operators, and scripts. You also have the ability to create mathematical structures such as integrals and functions.

# Formatting a SmartArt Graphic

Though you can use styles and themes to format a SmartArt graphic, you still may need to refine individual aspects of the graphic to make it look exactly the way you want it to look. You can use the commands on the SmartArt Tools Format tab to change shape styles, fills, outlines, and effects. You can also convert text within the SmartArt graphic to WordArt and format the text using any of the WordArt formatting commands. Individual shapes in the SmartArt graphic can be made larger or smaller, or altered into a different shape altogether. You continue working on the SmartArt graphic on Slide 3 by adjusting four shapes, adding pictures to shapes, and adjusting text in the graphic.

## STEPS

1. **Click the SmartArt graphic, click the SmartArt Tools Format tab on the Ribbon, then click the shape above the Tour Sites shape**

   The shape behind the picture icon is selected.

2. **Click the Change Shape button in the Shapes group, then click Round Diagonal Corner Rectangle (the last shape in the Rectangles section)**

   The form of the shape changes.

3. **Click the shape above the Package Details shape, press and hold [Ctrl], click the remaining two shapes, release [Ctrl], press [F4], then click in a blank area of the SmartArt graphic**

   All four small shapes now have a new shape as shown in Figure G-5.

4. **Click the picture icon 🖼 in the first shape on the left**

   The Insert Picture dialog box opens.

5. **Locate and click the file PPT G-2.jpg in the drive and folder where you store your Data Files, then click Insert**

   The picture is placed in the shape. Notice the picture takes on the contour of the shape.

6. **Click the 🖼 above the Package Details shape, insert the file PPT G-3.jpg, click the next 🖼, insert the file PPT G-4.jpg, click the last 🖼, then insert the file PPT G-5.jpg**

   All four shapes have pictures in them.

7. **Click a blank area inside the SmartArt graphic, then drag the left or right sizing handles to center the graphic in the white space on the slide**

   The SmartArt graphic fills the white area on the slide.

8. **Click a blank area of the slide, save your work, then click OK in the privacy warning message box**

   Compare your screen with Figure G-6.

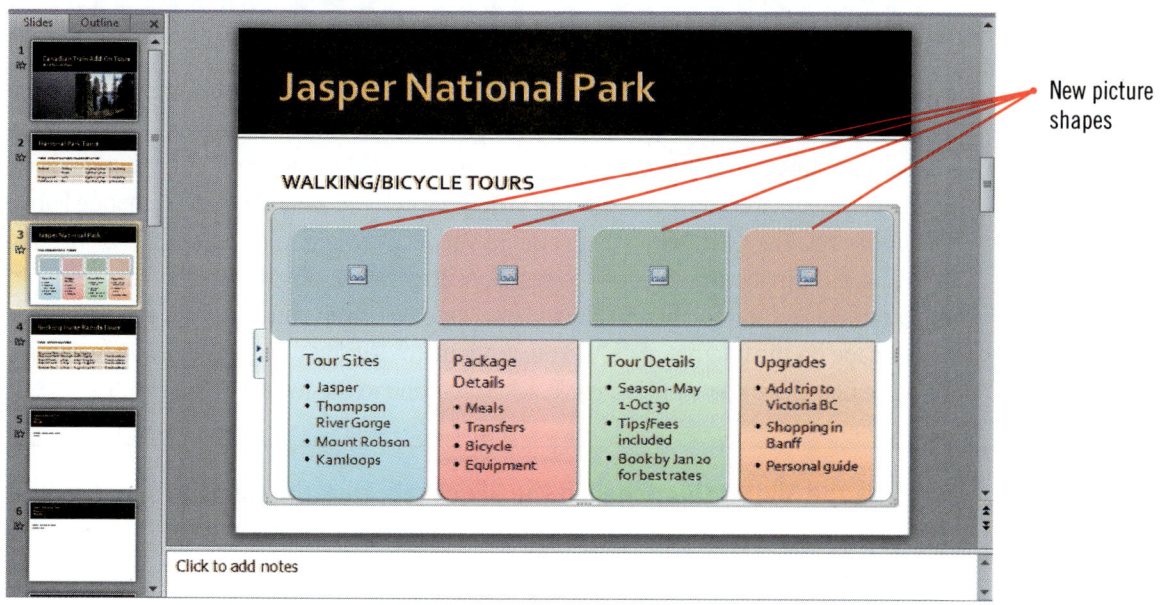

New picture shapes

Added pictures

## Saving a presentation in PDF and XPS file formats

In certain situations, such as when sharing sensitive or legal materials with others, you may find it necessary to save your presentation file in a fixed layout format. A **fixed layout format** is a specific file format that "locks" the file from future change and allows others only the ability to view or print the presentation. To save a presentation in one of these fixed formats, click the File tab on the Ribbon, click Save & Send, click Create PDF/XPS Document, then click Create a PDF/ XPS. The Publish as PDF or XPS dialog box opens. Select the appropriate file type in the Save as type list box, choose other options (optimization), then publish your presentation in a fixed layout format. To view a fixed layout format presentation, you need appropriate viewer software that you can download from the Internet.

# Inserting Clip Art Video

In your presentation, you may want to use special effects to illustrate a point or capture the attention of your audience. You can do this by inserting an animated or digital video. Animated videos contain multiple images that stream together or move when you run a slide show to give the illusion of motion. PowerPoint animated videos, also known as **clip art videos**, are stored as Graphics Interchange Format (GIF) files in the Clip Organizer. The **Clip Organizer** contains various drawings, photographs, clip art, sounds, and animated GIFs that you can insert into your presentation. **Digital video** is live action captured in digital format by a video camera. You can embed or link a digital video file from your hard drive or link a digital video file from a Web page on the Internet. You continue to develop your presentation by inserting a clip art video from the Clip Organizer showing backpackers walking in the forest.

## STEPS

1. **Click the Slide 2 thumbnail in the Slides tab, click the Insert tab on the Ribbon, click the Video list arrow in the Media group, then click Clip Art Video**
   The Clip Art task pane opens and displays clip art videos.

2. **Type backpacking in the Search for text box, then click Go**
   PowerPoint searches for backpacking clip art video.

3. **Scroll down the Clip Art task pane, if necessary, until you see the thumbnail of the backpackers shown in Figure G-7, then click the thumbnail**
   The backpacking clip art video appears in the center of the slide.

4. **Click the Clip Art task pane Close button** ✖
   The Clip Art task pane closes, and the Picture Tools Format tab is open on the Ribbon.

5. **Right-click the clip art video, then click Size and Position on the shortcut menu**
   The Format Picture dialog box opens.

6. **In the Scale section double-click the number 100 in the Height text box, type 300, then click Position in the left pane**
   The clip art video increases in size by 200 percent.

7. **Select the number in the Horizontal text box, type 6.2, press [Tab] twice, type 5.2 in the Vertical text box, then click Close**
   The clip art video moves to a new location at the bottom of the slide. The clip would look good with a soft edge effect from the Picture Effects gallery.

8. **Click the Picture Effects button in the Picture Styles group, point to Soft Edges, click 25 Point, then click a blank area of the slide**
   Compare your screen with Figure G-8. The clip art video won't begin unless you view it in Slide Show view.

9. **Click the Slide Show button** 🖳 **on the status bar, watch the video for a few seconds, press [Esc], save your work, then click OK in the privacy warning message box**

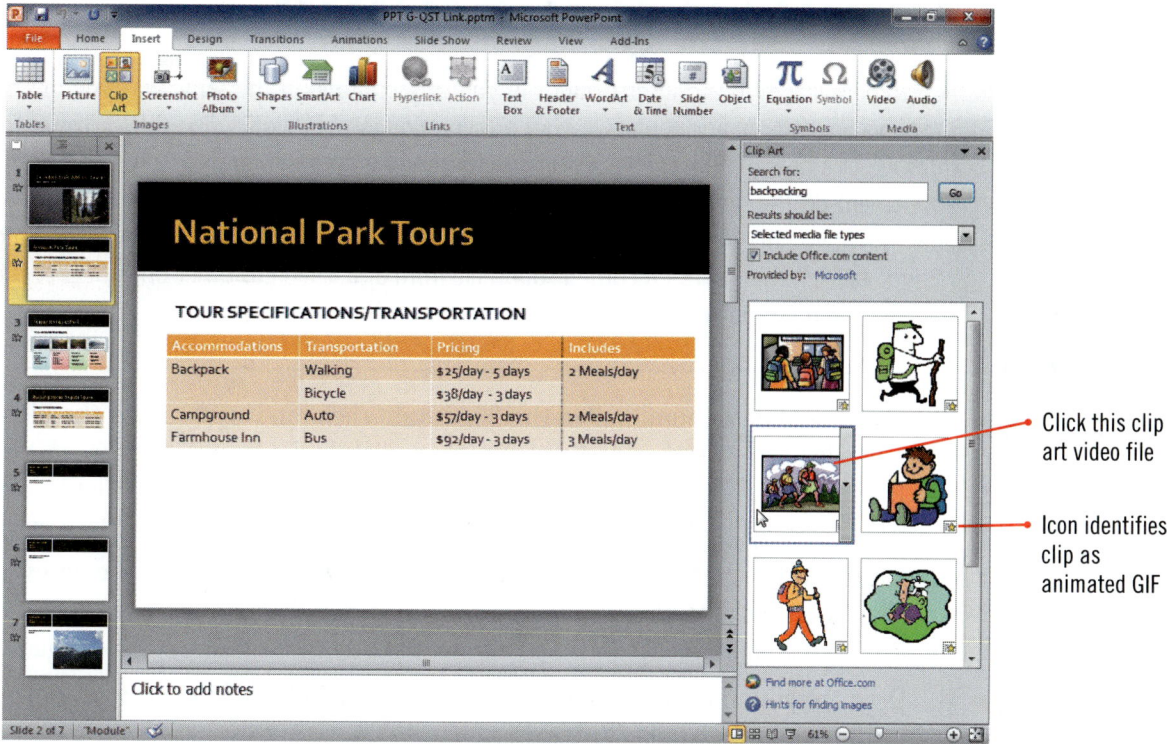

Click this clip art video file

Icon identifies clip as animated GIF

**FIGURE G-8:** Slide showing formatted clip art video

Modified clip art video

## Inserting and editing digital video

You can insert digital videos from files you have stored on your hard drive, any storage media, the Microsoft Web site, or other sources on the Internet. To insert a video on a PowerPoint slide, click the Insert tab, then click the Video list arrow in the Media group. Click either the Video from File option or the Video from Web Site option. Clicking the Video from File option opens the Insert Video dialog box where you can locate and insert a video file. Clicking the Video from Web Site option opens the Insert Video from Web Site dialog box. Use this dialog box to paste the embed code for the video you want to link from the Internet. To link a video from the Internet you must have a video file's embed code; otherwise, you cannot link the video file to a presentation. After you watch your video, you can use editing tools to trim beginning or ending portions of the video. You can also add a timed fade effect to the start or end of the video.

# Inserting a Sound

PowerPoint allows you to insert sounds in your presentation in the same way you insert clip art video or digital video. You can add sounds to your presentation from files on a disk, the Microsoft Clip Organizer, the Internet, or a network drive. The primary use of sound in a presentation is to provide emphasis to a slide or an element on the slide. For example, if you are creating a presentation about an Idaho raft tour on the Snake River, you might consider inserting a rushing water sound on a slide showing a photograph of people rafting. 🎨🎨 You insert a recorded sound file from a satisfied customer on Slide 3 of the presentation to enhance the message on the slide.

## STEPS

**QUICK TIP**
To insert a sound from the Microsoft Clip Organizer, click the Audio list arrow, then click Clip Art Audio.

1. **Click the Slide 3 thumbnail in the Slides tab, click the Insert tab on the Ribbon, click the Audio list arrow in the Media group, then click Audio from File**

   The Insert Audio dialog box opens. Common sound formats you can insert into a presentation include Windows audio files (Wave Form) (wav), MP3 audio files (mp3), and Windows Media Audio files (wma).

2. **Locate and click the file PPT G-6.wma in the drive and folder where you store your Data Files, then click Insert**

   A sound icon with an audio control bar appears in the center of the slide as shown Figure G-9.

**TROUBLE**
If the sound does not play, see your instructor or technical support person for help.

3. **Drag the sound icon 🔈 to the right of Walking/Bicycle Tours, then click the Play/Pause button ▷ in the audio control bar**

   The sound icon is moved off the SmartArt graphic and plays one time through. After hearing the audio play, you decide to trim the start point to cut out the laughing at the beginning.

4. **Click the Audio Tools Playback tab on the Ribbon, click the Trim Audio button in the Editing group, then drag the dialog box down the slide below the sound icon**

   The Trim Audio dialog box opens as shown in Figure G-10. Notice on the audio timeline the start point (green marker) and the end point (red marker), which identify the beginning and end of the audio. The audio is 19.551 seconds long.

5. **Click the Play button ▶ in the Trim Audio dialog box, watch the audio on the sound timeline, then drag the start point ▌ to the right until 00:03.126 appears above the sound timeline**

   The audio will now start at this point when played. The end of the audio needs to be changed also.

6. **Click the End Time down arrow until 00:17.200 appears as shown in Figure G-11, click OK, then click ▷ in the audio control bar**

   The audio now plays between the new start and end points. By default, the audio plays when you click the sound icon during a slide show.

**QUICK TIP**
You can add a bookmark to an audio clip that identifies a specific point in time. You can use bookmarks to manually start or end an audio or jump to a precise point in the audio.

7. **Click the Start button in the Audio Options group, then click Automatically**

   The audio will now run automatically as soon as the slide appears in Slide Show view.

8. **Click the Slide Show button 🖵 on the status bar, then listen to the audio**

   Notice that the sound icon appears during the slide show. You can hide the sound icon during a slide show by clicking the Hide During Show check box in the Audio Options group.

9. **Press [Esc], click a blank area of the slide, then save your changes**

**FIGURE G-9:** Slide showing inserted sound

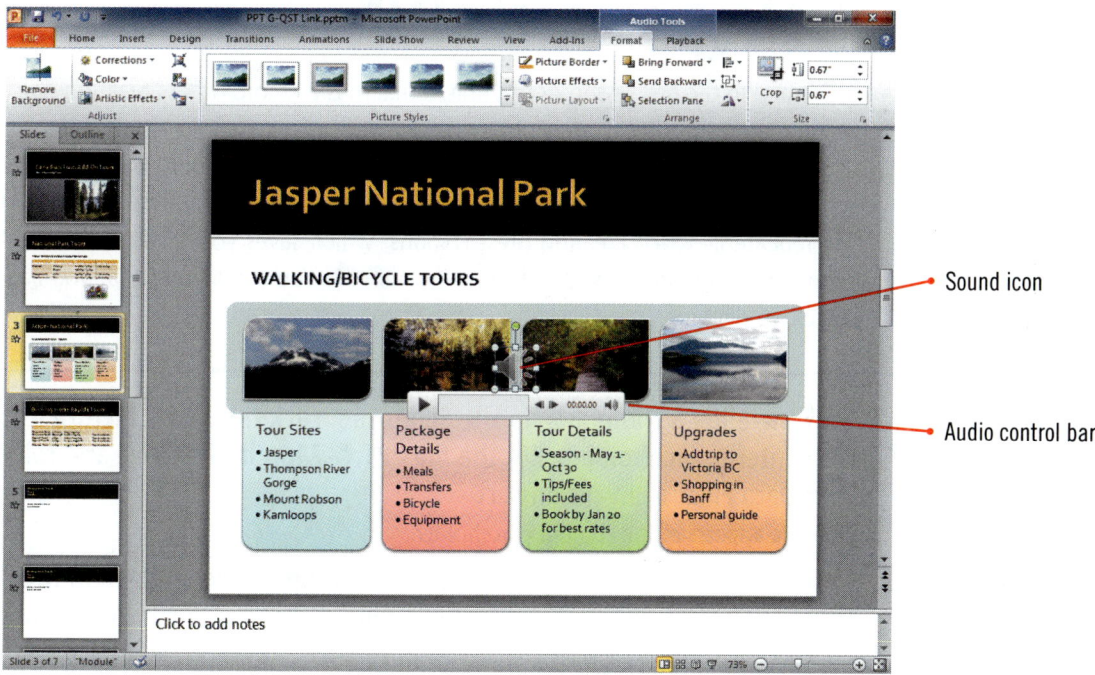

Sound icon

Audio control bar

**FIGURE G-10:** Trim Audio dialog box

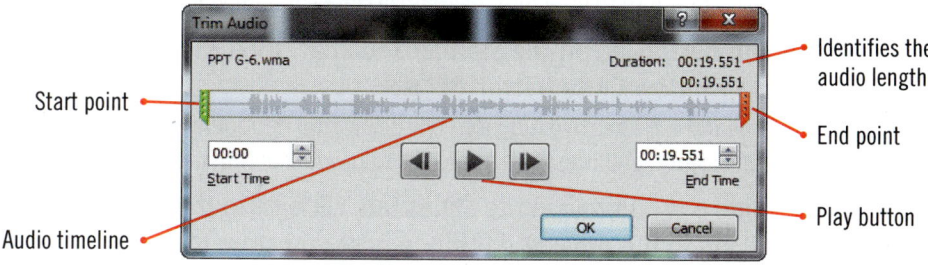

Start point

Audio timeline

Identifies the audio length

End point

Play button

**FIGURE G-11:** Trim Audio dialog box showing trimmed audio

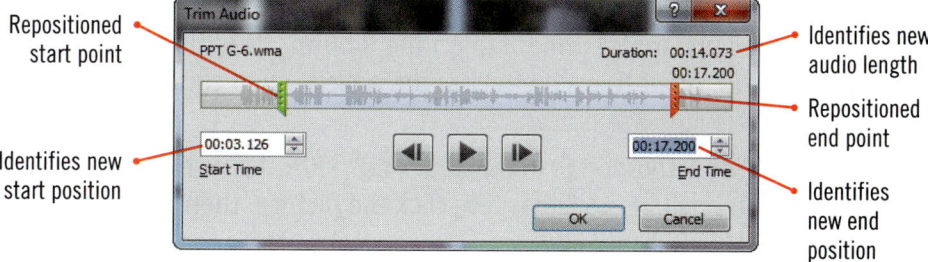

Repositioned start point

Identifies new start position

Identifies new audio length

Repositioned end point

Identifies new end position

## Recording a voice narration on a slide

If your computer has speakers, a sound card, and a microphone, you can record a voice narration and then play it during a slide show. To record a narration, click the Insert tab on the Ribbon, click the Audio list arrow in the Media group, then click Record Audio. The Record Sound dialog box opens. To start recording, click the Record button in the dialog box, then click the Stop button when you are finished.

A sound icon appears on the slide. Narration recordings and other sounds are embedded in the presentation and will increase the PowerPoint file size. You can preview a narration in Normal view by pointing to the sound icon on the slide, then clicking the Play/Pause button in the audio control bar.

# Using Macros

As you learned in the first lesson of this unit, a macro is a recording of an action or a set of actions that you use to automate tasks. The contents of a macro consist of a series of command codes that you create in the Visual Basic for Applications programming language using Microsoft Visual Basic, which you can access through the Developer tab in PowerPoint. You can use macros to automate almost any action that you perform repeatedly when creating presentations, which saves you time and effort. Any presentation with the .pptm file extension is saved with a macro. You use macros that you already created to format and place two pictures.

## STEPS

**QUICK TIP**
To add the Developer tab to the Ribbon, click the File tab on the Ribbon, click Options, click Customize Ribbon in the left pane, click the Developer check box in the Main Tabs list box, then click OK.

1. **Click the Slide 5 thumbnail in the Slides tab, click the Insert Picture from File icon** 🖻 **in the content placeholder, click the file PPT G-7.jpg in the drive and folder where you store your Data Files, then click Insert**

   A picture appears in the content placeholder.

2. **Click the View tab on the Ribbon, then click the Macros button in the Macro group**

   The Macro dialog box opens displaying the two macros attached to this presentation file.

3. **Click Module2.PictureReduction in the Macro name list, then click Edit**

   The Microsoft Visual Basic for Applications window opens displaying two small windows as shown in Figure G-12. Each window represents a separate macro. Each macro is designed to modify the size of a picture and place it in a specific place on the slide. The difference between the two macros is that the Module2 macro unlocks the aspect ratio so that pictures of any size can be modified within the designated parameters.

4. **Click the Run button** ▶ **on the Standard toolbar, then click the Microsoft Visual Basic for Applications window Close button** ✖

   The macro runs and performs two functions on the picture: It modifies the size of the picture to specific width and height dimensions, and it moves the picture to precise coordinates on the slide.

5. **Click the Slide 6 thumbnail in the Slides tab, click** 🖻 **in the content placeholder, click the file PPT G-8.jpg in the drive and folder where you store your Data Files, then click Insert**

   A picture appears in the content placeholder.

**QUICK TIP**
To learn more about macros and the Visual Basic for Applications programming language, click the Visual Basic button on the Developer tab to open the Visual Basic window, then click the Help button.

6. **Click the View tab on the Ribbon, click the Macros button in the Macro group, click Module2.PictureReduction in the Macro name list, then click Run**

   The macro runs and modifies the picture size and position on the slide.

7. **Click the Picture Tools Format tab on the Ribbon, click the Artistic Effects button in the Adjust group, point to each effect in the gallery, then click Plastic Wrap**

   The picture is formatted with an artistic effect.

8. **Click the Slide 5 thumbnail in the Slides tab, click the picture, then press [F4], click the Slide 7 thumbnail in the Slides tab, click the picture, then press [F4]**

   All of the pictures at the end of the presentation now have the same artistic effect.

9. **Click a blank area of the slide, then save your work**

   Compare your screen to Figure G-13.

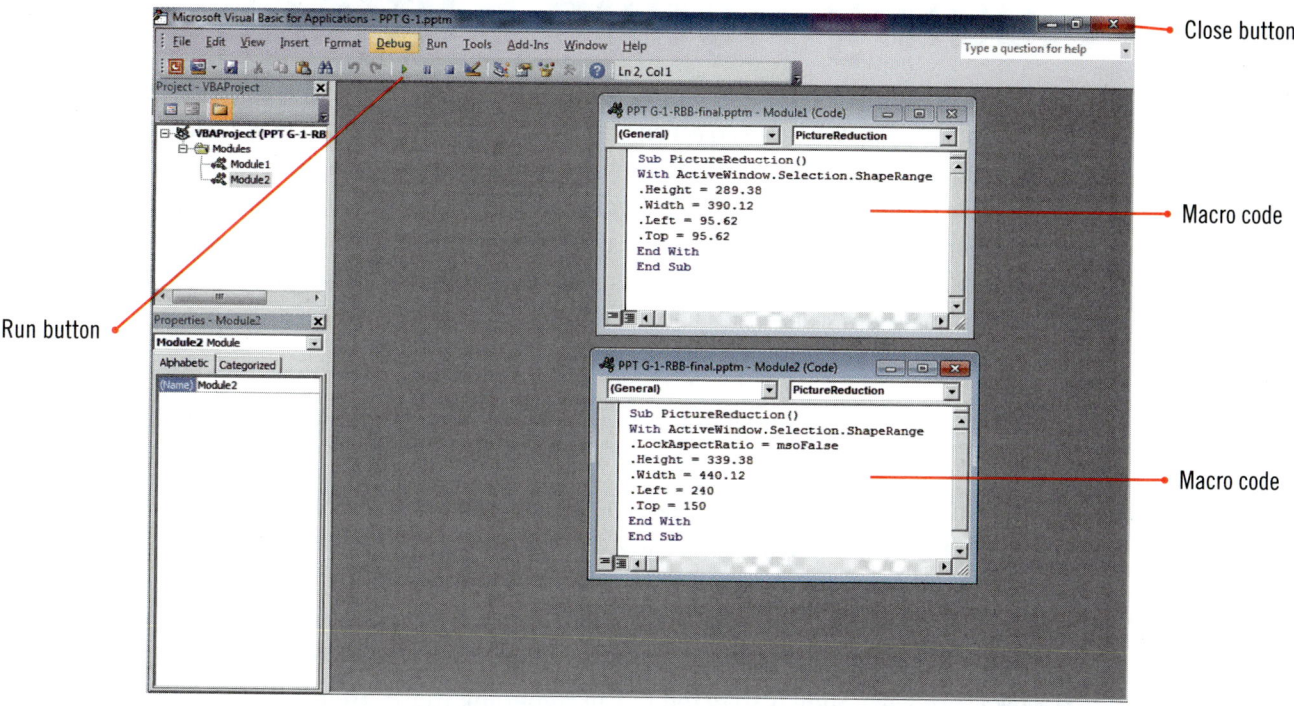

**FIGURE G-12:** Visual Basic window

Run button — (points to Run button)
Close button — (points to close button)
Macro code — (points to Module1 code)
Macro code — (points to Module2 code)

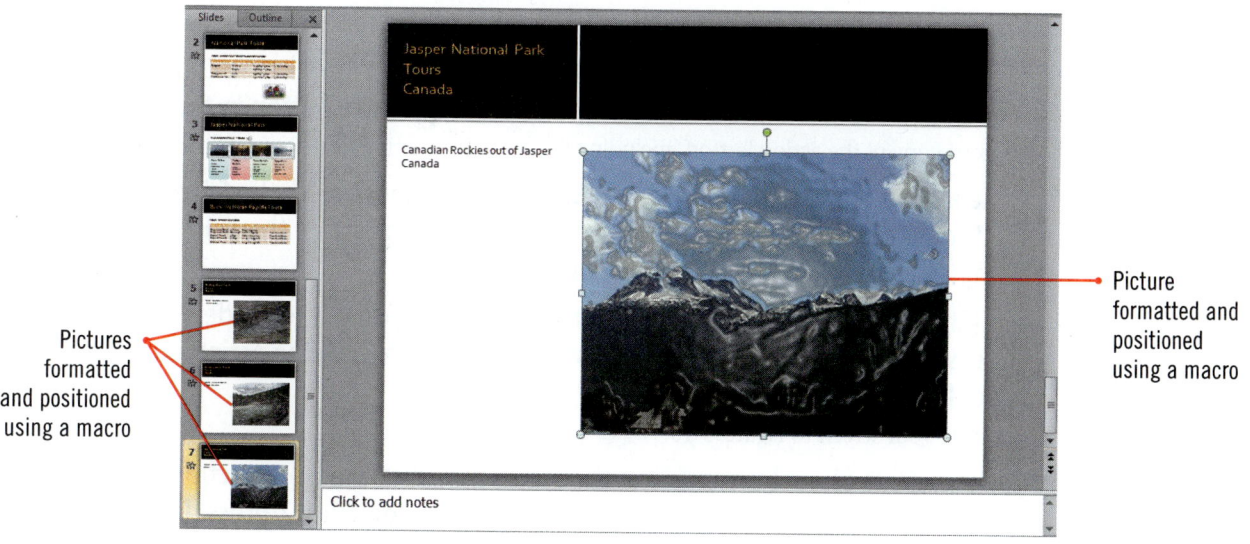

**FIGURE G-13:** Screen showing inserted picture

Pictures formatted and positioned using a macro

Picture formatted and positioned using a macro

## Macro security

There are certain risks involved when you enable macros on your computer. The macros used in this lesson are simple commands that automate the size and relative position of a picture on a slide; however, hackers can introduce harmful viruses or other malicious programs into your computer using macros. By default, PowerPoint disables macros when you open a presentation file that includes macros to prevent possible damage to your computer. To understand PowerPoint security settings and how PowerPoint checks for harmful macros, click the Macro Security button on the Developer tab, or click the File tab, click Options, then click Trust Center in the left pane. The bottom line with macros is if you can't trust the source of the macro, do not enable them.

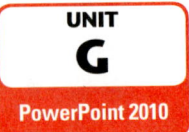
# Adding Action Buttons

An **action button** is an interactive button that you create from the Shapes gallery to perform a specific task. For example, you can create an action button to play a video or a sound, or to link to another slide in your presentation. Action buttons can also link to an Internet address on the Web, a different presentation, or another file created in another program. You can also run a macro or another program using an action button. Action buttons are commonly used in self-running presentations and presentations published on the Web. You finish working on this presentation by adding action buttons to each slide, which will allow you to move from slide to slide and back to the first slide.

## STEPS

1. **Click the Slide 1 thumbnail in the Slides tab, then click the Home tab on the Ribbon**
   Slide 1 appears in the Slide pane.

**QUICK TIP**

Any shape in the Shapes gallery as well as most other objects can be an action button. Click the shape or object, click the Insert tab, click the Action button in the Links group, then select an action.

2. **Click the Shapes button in the Drawing group to open the Shapes gallery, click Action Button: Forward or Next ▷ in the Action Buttons section, press and hold [Shift], drag to create a button as shown in Figure G-14, then release [Shift]**
   A small action button appears on the slide, and the Action Settings dialog box opens. Pressing [Shift] while you create a shape maintains the shape's proportions as you change its size.

3. **Make sure Next Slide is selected in the Hyperlink to list, then click OK**
   The dialog box closes. The action button now has an action, in this case, moving to the next slide.

4. **Click the Drawing Tools Format tab on the Ribbon, click the More button ▾ in the Shape Styles group, then click Light 1 Outline, Colored Fill – Red, Accent 6 in the 3rd row**
   The action button is easier to see on the slide.

5. **Drag the action button to the lower-left corner of the slide**

**QUICK TIP**

Use the arrow keys on your keyboard to nudge the action button into place. You can also press [Alt] while dragging the action button to nudge it into place.

6. **Click the Home tab on the Ribbon, click the Copy button 🗐 ▾ in the Clipboard group, click the Slide 2 thumbnail in the Slides tab, then click the Paste button in the Clipboard group**
   An exact copy of the action button, including the associated action, is placed on Slide 2.

7. **Paste a copy of the action button on Slides 3, 4, 5, and 6, click the Slide 7 thumbnail in the Slides tab, click the Shapes button in the Drawing group, then click Action Button: Home 🏠 in the Action Buttons section**

8. **Use [Shift] to create a similar sized action button as you did for Slide 1, make sure First Slide is selected in the Hyperlink to list, click OK, then drag the action button to the lower-left corner of the slide**
   Compare your screen to Figure G-15.

9. **Click the Slide Show button 🖵 on the status bar, click the Home action button, click the action buttons to move from slide to slide, then on Slide 7 press [Esc] to end the slide show**
   The pointer changes to 👆 when you click each action button.

10. **Add your name to the slide footer, save your changes, submit your presentation to your instructor, click the File tab on the Ribbon, then click Close to close the presentation but do not exit PowerPoint**

Action Settings
dialog box

Action button

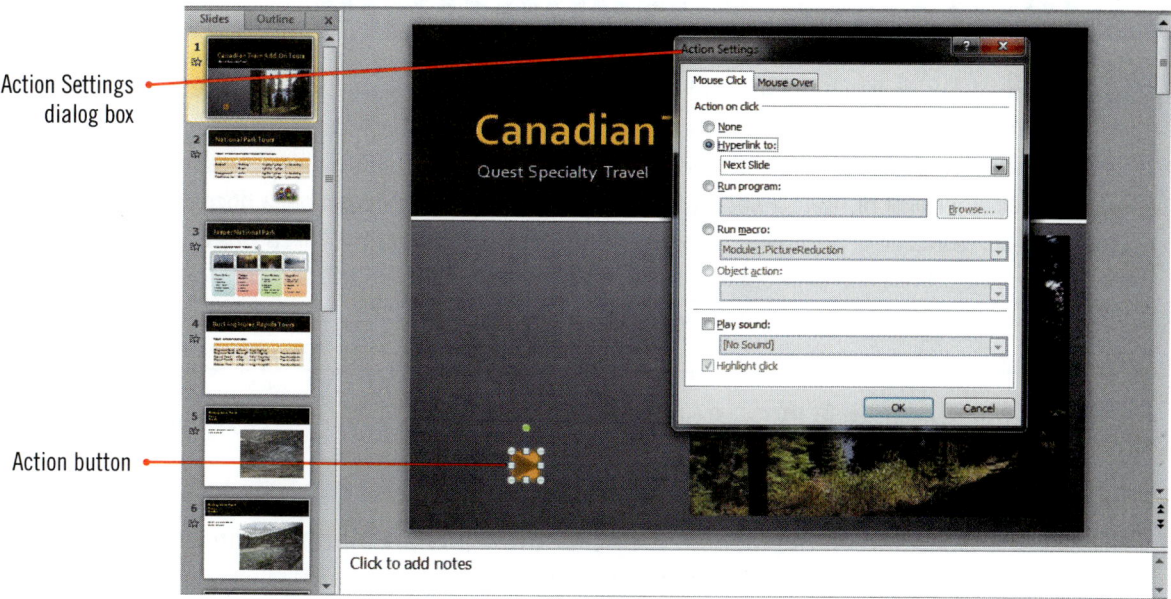

Home action
button

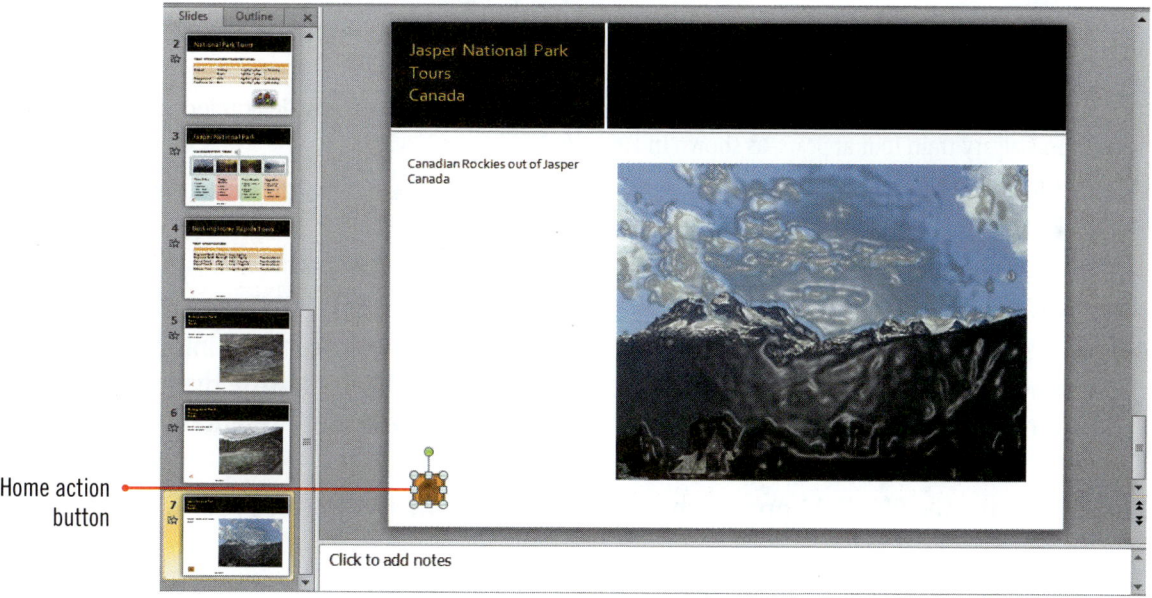

## Saving slides as graphics

You can save PowerPoint slides as graphics and later use them in other presentations, in graphics programs, and on Web pages. Display the slide you want to save, click the File tab, then click Save As. In the Save As dialog box, click the Save as type list arrow, select the desired graphics format, then name the file. Graphics format choices include JPEG file Interchange Format (*.jpg), TIFF Tag Image File Format (*.tif), and Device Independent Bitmap (*.bmp). Click Save, then click the desired option when the alert box appears asking if you want to save all the slides or only the current slide.

# Inserting a Hyperlink

While creating a presentation, there might be a circumstance where you want to view a document that either won't fit on the slide or is too detailed for your presentation. In these cases, you can insert a **hyperlink**, a specially formatted word, phrase, graphic, or drawn object that you click during a slide show to "jump to," or display, another slide or PowerPoint presentation in your current presentation; a document from another program, like Word; or a Web page. A hyperlinked object is similar to a linked object because you can modify the object in its source program. You add two hyperlinks to the primary presentation you have been working on that provide more detail on the Jasper bicycle tour.

1. **Open the presentation PPT G-9.pptx from the drive and folder where you store your Data Files, then save the presentation as PPT G-Final.pptx**

**QUICK TIP**

Links can also be established between slides of the same presentation, a new presentation, an e-mail address, or any Web page.

2. **Click the Slide 6 thumbnail in the Slides tab, select Route highlights in the text object, click the Insert tab on the Ribbon, then click the Hyperlink button in the Links group**

   The Insert Hyperlink dialog box opens. The Existing File or Web Page button is selected in the Link to: pane, and the Current Folder button is selected in the Look in pane.

3. **Click the file PPT G-10.docx in the drive and folder where you store your Data Files, click OK, then click in a blank area of the slide**

   Now that you have made Route highlights a hyperlink to the file PPT G-10.docx, the text is formatted in a green color and is underlined, which is how a hyperlink is formatted in this theme. It's important to test any hyperlink you create.

4. **Click the Slide Show button 🖵 on the status bar, point to Route highlights, notice the pointer change to 🖑, then click Route highlights**

   Microsoft Word opens, and the Word document containing a detailed description of the Vancouver-to-Calgary train tour appears, as shown in Figure G-16.

5. **Click the down scroll arrow and read the document, then click the Word window Close button ⬛ˣ**

   The PowerPoint slide reappears in Slide Show view. The hyperlink is now a light brown, the color for followed hyperlinks in this theme, indicating that the hyperlink has been selected or viewed.

**QUICK TIP**

To edit, open, copy, or remove a hyperlink, right-click the hyperlink, then click the appropriate command on the shortcut menu.

6. **Press [Esc], click the Slide 8 thumbnail in the Slides tab, right-click the Information action button, click Hyperlink, click the Hyperlink to option button, click the Hyperlink to list arrow, click the down scroll arrow, then click Other PowerPoint Presentation**

   The Hyperlink to Other PowerPoint Presentation dialog box opens.

7. **Click the file PPT G-11.pptx in the drive and folder where you store your Data Files, then click OK**

   The Hyperlink to Slide dialog box opens. You can choose which slides you want to link to.

8. **Click OK to link to Slide 1, click OK to close the Action Settings dialog box, click 🖵, click the Information action button, click the action buttons to view the slides in the presentation, press [Esc] to end the slide show, then press [Esc] again**

   The slide show ends. Both hyperlinks work correctly.

9. **Add your name to the notes and handouts footer, save your changes, then click the Slide Sorter button 🔲 on the status bar**

   Compare your screen to Figure G-17.

10. **Submit your presentation to your instructor, close the presentation, then exit PowerPoint**

**FIGURE G-16:** Linked Word document

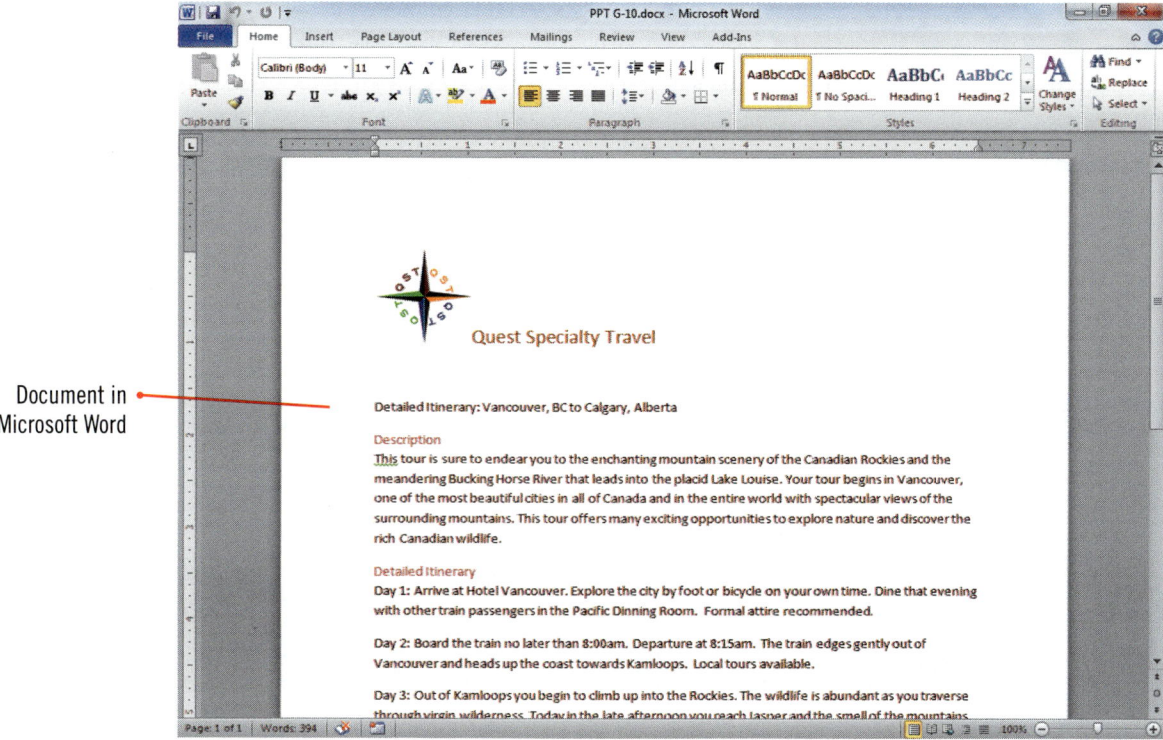

Document in
Microsoft Word

**FIGURE G-17:** Final presentation in Slide Sorter view

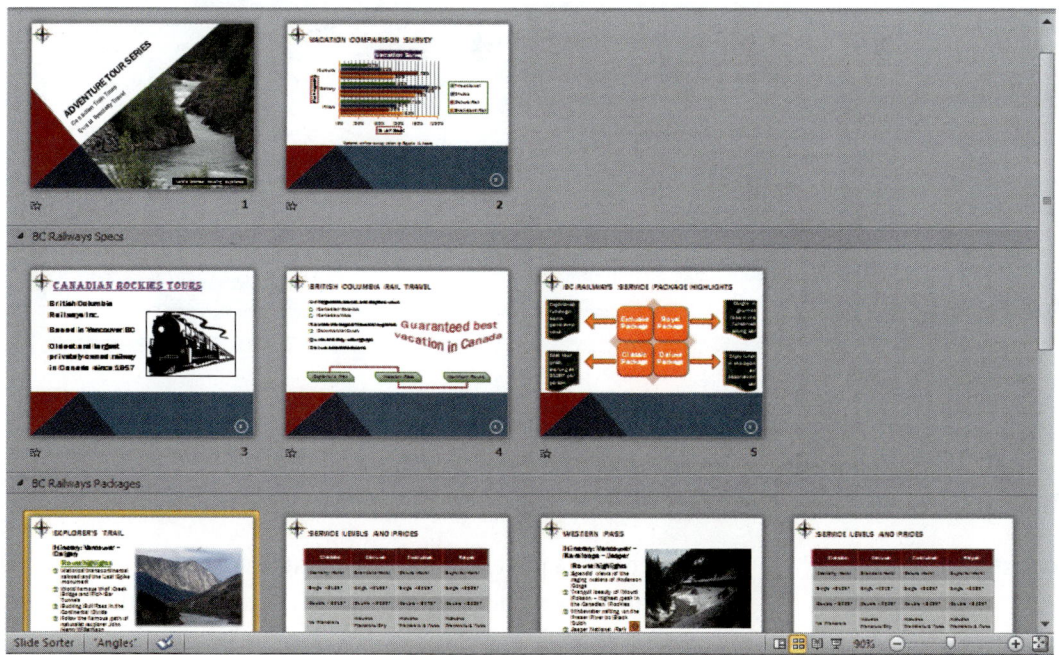

# Practice

## Concepts Review

For current SAM information, including versions and content details, visit SAM Central (http://www.cengage.com/samcentral). If you have a SAM user profile, you may have access to hands-on instruction, practice, and assessment of the skills covered in this unit. Since various versions of SAM are supported throughout the life of this text, check with your instructor for the correct instructions and URL/Web site for accessing assignments.

**Label each element of the PowerPoint window shown in Figure G-18.**

FIGURE G-18

**Match each of the terms with the statement that best describes its function.**

9. **Equation button**

10. **.pptm**

11. **Animated video**

12. **Macro**

13. **Action button**

14. **Hyperlink**

a. Identifies a presentation file with attached macros

b. A file that contains multiple images streamed together that move during a slide show

c. Click to create mathematical integrals and functions

d. An interactive shape that performs a specific task when clicked

e. A formatted word or graphic that you can click to jump to a Web page

f. A set of actions you use to automate tasks

**Select the best answer from the list of choices.**

15. A _____ format is a specific file format that "locks" the file from future changes.
    a. movie
    b. GIF
    c. macro enabled
    d. fixed layout

16. Which statement best describes the function of a hyperlink in PowerPoint?
    a. A button clicked in a table to start the slide show
    b. Click during a slide show to display an Excel file
    c. Used for animation
    d. Enables a macro

17. Which of the following combines content with an illustrative diagram?
    a. Hyperlink
    b. Table
    c. SmartArt
    d. Action button

18. What is an animated GIF file?
    a. Multiple images streamed together
    b. A hyperlink
    c. A sound
    d. A digital movie

19. According to the book, a _____ is live action captured in a digital format.
    a. GIF file
    b. video
    c. hyperlink
    d. macro

20. A macro is essentially a series of _____ that you create in Visual Basic for Applications.
    a. action buttons
    b. file extensions
    c. linked files
    d. command codes

# Skills Review

1. **Create custom tables.**
   a. Start PowerPoint, open the presentation PPT G-12.pptm from the drive and folder where you store your Data Files, click the Enable Content button, then save it as **PPT G-Cheese Industry**.
   b. Go to Slide 5, select the table, click the Table Tools Design tab, click the More button in the Table Styles group, then click the Medium Style 1 – Accent 3 in the Medium section.
   c. Click the Pen Weight button in the Draw Borders group, select 2¼ pt, then apply the new line style to the horizontal border for the first row.
   d. Apply the 2¼-pt line style to the vertical border lines between the cells in the first row, then click the Draw Table button.
   e. Select the table, open the Table Tools Layout tab, click the Cell Margins button in the Alignment group, then click Wide.
   f. Click anywhere in the upper-left cell, click the Select button in the Table group, click Select Row, then click the Center button in the Alignment group.
   g. Click anywhere in the bottom row, then click the Insert Below button in the Rows & Columns group.
   h. Click the left cell of the new row, type **Tomme de Savoie**, press [Tab], type **Valencay**, then save your changes.

2. **Design a SmartArt graphic.**
   a. Go to Slide 4, click the SmartArt graphic, then click the SmartArt Tools Design tab.
   b. Click the More button in the Layouts group, then click Vertical Picture Accent List in the fourth row.
   c. Open the Text pane if it is closed, click the Add Shape list arrow in the Create Graphic group, then click Add Shape After.
   d. Type **Production**, press [Enter], click the Demote button in the Create Graphic group, type **Cow cheese 1.96 million tons**, press [Enter], type **Goat cheese 0.88 million tons**, press [Enter], type **Blue cheese 0.25 million tons**.
   e. Close the Text pane, click the Change Colors button in the SmartArt Styles group, then click Colorful Range – Accent Colors 5 to 6 in the Colorful section.
   f. Click the Right to Left button in the Create Graphic group.
   g. Resize and reposition the SmartArt graphic so it is centered on the slide, then save your changes.

# Skills Review (continued)

3. **Format a SmartArt graphic.**
   a. Click the SmartArt Tools Format tab, click the top circle shape in the SmartArt graphic, then click the Smaller button in the Shapes group.
   b. Use the Smaller button in the Shapes group to decrease the size of the two other circle shapes in the SmartArt graphic.
   c. Click the Insert picture icon in the bottom circle shape, then locate and insert the file PPT G-13.jpg from the drive and folder where you store your Data Files.
   d. Follow the above instructions and insert the file PPT G-13.jpg to the other two circle shapes, then save your changes.

4. **Insert clip art video.**
   a. Go to Slide 7, click the Insert tab on the Ribbon, click the Video list arrow in the Media group, then click Clip Art Video to open the Clip Art task pane.
   b. Insert a clip art video of your choosing on the slide. Type the word **e-mail** to search for an appropriate animated GIF.
   c. Resize and reposition the GIF file as necessary.
   d. Click the Picture Effects button in the Picture Styles group, then apply an effect of your choice.
   e. Preview the clip art video in Slide Show view, close the Clip Art task pane, then save your presentation.

5. **Insert a sound.**
   a. Go to Slide 2.
   b. Click the Insert tab, click the Audio list arrow in the Media group, then click Audio from File.
   c. Locate and insert the sound file PPT G-14.wav from the drive and folder where you store your Data Files.
   d. Preview the sound, set the sound to start automatically during a slide show, then drag the sound icon below the map graphic of France.
   e. Use the Trim Audio dialog box to change the end point of the audio clip to 00:01.700.
   f. Click the Hide During Show check box in the Audio Options group, click the Slide Show button on the status bar, review the slide, press [Esc], then save your presentation.

6. **Use macros.**
   a. Go to Slide 6, click the Insert tab on the Ribbon, then click the Picture button in the Images group.
   b. Locate the file PPT G-15.jpg in the drive and folder where you store your Data Files, then insert the file.
   c. Click the View tab on the Ribbon, click the Macros button, then click Run in the Macro dialog box.
   d. Drag the picture to the center of the blank area of the slide above the text at the bottom of the slide. Use the guides to help you center the picture.
   e. Click the Picture Tools Format tab on the Ribbon, click the More button in the Picture Styles group, click Metal Frame in the top row, then save your work.

7. **Add action buttons.**
   a. Go to Slide 1, click the Shapes button in the Drawing group, then click Action Button: Forward or Next.
   b. Draw a small button, click OK in the Action Settings dialog box, then position the button in the upper-left corner of the slide.
   c. Click the Drawing Tools Format tab on the Ribbon, click the More button in the Shape Styles group, then click Intense Effect – Light Yellow, Accent 4 in the bottom row.
   d. Copy and paste the action button on Slides 2–7.
   e. Go to Slide 8, click the Shapes button, click Action Button: Beginning, draw a small button, click OK, then drag the button to the upper-left corner of the slide.
   f. Go to Slide 7, click the action button, click the Format Painter button in the Clipboard group, click Slide 8, then click the action button.
   g. Run the slide show from Slide 1 and test the action buttons, then save your work.

8. **Insert a hyperlink.**
   a. Go to Slide 6, then select the words **Fredrick Amen** in the text object.
   b. Click the Insert tab on the Ribbon, click the Hyperlink button, locate the file PPT G-16.docx in the drive and folder where you store your Data Files, then click OK.

# Skills Review (continued)

c. Click in the Notes pane, then type **The hyperlink opens Fred's cheese review of the 2013 French Camembert**.

d. Open Slide Show view, click the hyperlink, read the review, then click the Word window Close button.

e. Press [Esc], then add your name as a footer to the slides.

f. Check the spelling in the presentation, view the presentation in Slide Show view from Slide 1.

g. Make any necessary changes. The completed presentation is shown in Figure G-19.

h. Submit your presentation to your instructor, then save and close the presentation.

**FIGURE G-19**

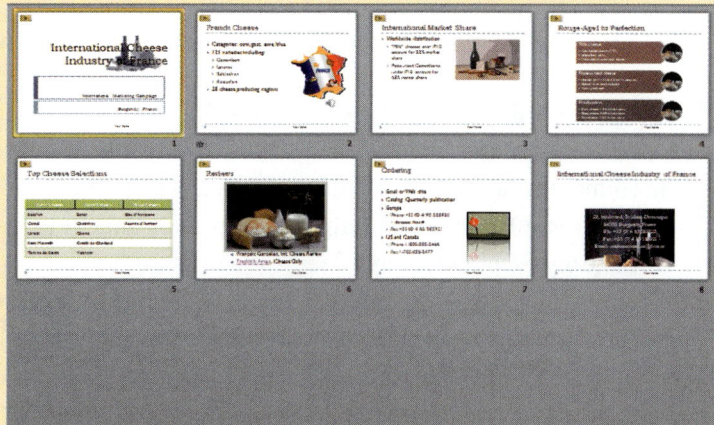

## Independent Challenge 1

Milsap Brothers Engineering is a mechanical and industrial design company that specializes in designing manufacturing plants around the world. As a company financial analyst, you need to investigate and report on a possible contract to design and build a large manufacturing plant in China.

a. Open the file PPT G-17.pptx, then save it as **PPT G-China**.

b. On Slide 3, apply the table style Themed Style 1 – Accent 5, then draw a dotted line down the center of the table using the Pen Style button.

c. Click in the top row of the table, insert a row above the top row, type **Line Item** in the left cell, then type **Budget** in the right cell.

d. Click the Overhead/Benefits cell, split the cell into two columns and one row, then move the word **Benefits** to the new cell and delete the slash.

e. Create a new SmartArt graphic on Slide 4 using the following process information: **Planning and Design, Site Acquisition and Preparation, Underground Construction, Above-ground Construction**, and **Finish and Building Completion**.

f. Change the colors of the graphic to a colorful theme, then apply a 3-D style.

g. Change the shape of at least one shape in the SmartArt graphic using the Change Shape button, then click the Right to Left button in the Create Graphic group on the SmartArt Tools Design tab.

h. Add your name as a footer on the slides, then save your changes.

### Advanced Challenge Exercise

■ Create a new slide using the Title and Content slide layout, type **Project Organization** in the title placeholder, then create an hierarchy chart SmartArt graphic.

■ Fill the text boxes with the following job titles: **Project Manager, Project Foreman, Design Manager,** and **Project Coordinator**.

■ Click the top shape, click the Layout button in the Create Graphic group, then click Left Hanging.

■ Format the graphic by adding a new style and color theme, make any other necessary changes, then save the presentation as **Chinese Plant ACE**.

i. Check the presentation spelling, view the presentation in Slide Show view, submit your presentation to your instructor, then close the presentation and exit PowerPoint.

# Independent Challenge 2

You work for The Feldman Group, a large investment banking firm in Omaha, Nebraska. Feldman is considering buying Waxby Financial Services, a smaller investment company in Oklahoma City. As part of the company financial operations team, you need to present some projections regarding the purchase to a special committee formed by Feldman to study the proposed deal.

**a.** Open the file PPT G-18.pptx from the drive and folder where you store your Data Files, then save it as **PPT G-Feldman**.

**b.** Format the table on Slide 3 first, apply a table style from the Light Style 2 styles section of the Table Styles gallery; next draw three 1½-pt dotted vertical cell separator lines in the table, and finally, click the First Column check box in the Table Style Options group.

**c.** Convert the text on Slide 5 to a SmartArt graphic using one of the List layouts.

**d.** Format the SmartArt graphic by applying an Accent 3 color theme, and then changing the SmartArt style to Subtle Effect.

**e.** Insert a clip art video on Slide 3. Use the word **profits** to search for an appropriate animated GIF.

**f.** Select the word **Waxby** on Slide 2, click the Insert tab on the Ribbon, click the Hyperlink button in the Links group, locate the file PPT G-19.pptx from the drive and folder where you store your Data Files, then click OK.

**g.** Add your name as a footer on the slides, check the spelling of the presentation, then save your changes.

**h.** View the presentation in Slide Show view, and click the hyperlink on Slide 2.

**i.** Submit your presentation to your instructor, close the presentation, then exit PowerPoint.

# Independent Challenge 3

You have been recently hired at Rinco Inc., a U.S. company that exports goods and services to companies in all parts of Asia, including Japan, Hong Kong, China, and the Philippines. One of your new responsibilities is to prepare short presentations on different subjects for use on the company Web site using data provided to you by others in the company.

**a.** Open the file PPT G-20.pptx from the drive and folder where you store your Data Files, then save it as **PPT G-Rinco**.

**b.** Add a design theme, background shading, or other objects to make your presentation look professional. Make adjustments to objects as necessary.

**c.** Convert the text on Slide 3 to a SmartArt graphic, then format the graphic using any of the formatting commands available.

**d.** Insert an appropriate clip art video on the last slide of the presentation.

**e.** Insert a sound on Slide 2. Use the word **harbor** to search for an appropriate sound.

**f.** Change the layout and format the charts on Slides 4 and 5.

**g.** Create, format, and position Forward action buttons on Slides 1–5.

**h.** Create, format, and position Back action buttons on Slides 2–6, then create, format, and position a Home action button on Slide 6.

**Advanced Challenge Exercise** *(Requirements: connected microphone, sound card, and speakers)*

- Prepare a narration for one or more slides, then produce a narration by using one of the following steps.
- **One slide:** To add a narration to one slide, go to the slide, click the Insert tab, click the Audio list arrow, click Record Audio, click the Record button in the Record Sound dialog box, record your narration, then click the Stop button to end the recording.
- **Multiple slides:** To add a narration to multiple slides while viewing a slide show, click the Slide Show tab, click the Record Slide Show button in the Set Up group, click Start Recording, record your narration, then click [Esc] to end the recording.

# Independent Challenge 3 (continued)

i. Add your name as a footer to the slides, check the spelling of the presentation, save your changes, then view the presentation in Slide Show view. See Figure G-20.

j. Submit your presentation to your instructor, close the presentation, then exit PowerPoint.

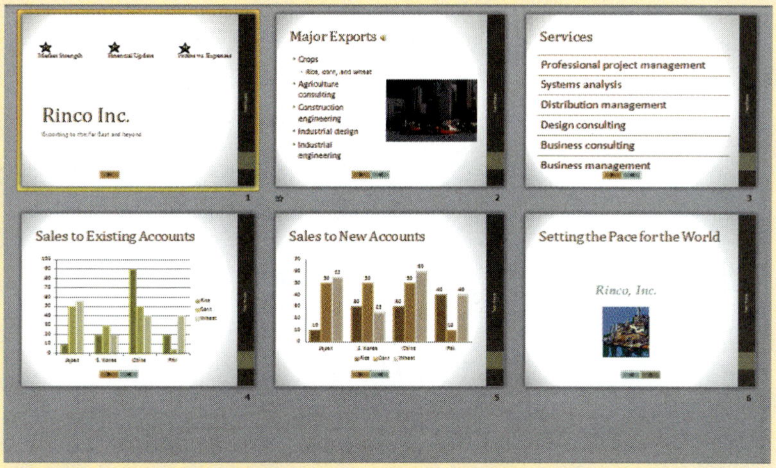

## Real Life Independent Challenge

One of the assignments in your business course at the university is to give a 15-minute presentation on any subject to the class. The goal of the

**FIGURE G-20**

assignment is for you to persuade the class (and your instructor) to make an informed decision about the subject you are presenting based on your ability to communicate the facts. You decide to create a presentation using pictures and other media to play in the background while you give your presentation.

To develop the content of this presentation:

- Choose your own subject matter, for example, a favorite hobby or sport.
- Use your own media clips (pictures, sounds, or video) on your computer. If you don't have your own media clips, you can search the Clip Organizer for appropriate clips.

a. Open the file PPT G-21.pptm from the drive and folder where you store your Data Files, then save it as **PPT G-Business**. Click the Enable Content button. The file PPT G-21.pptm has no content, but is macro-enabled.

b. Add your name, the date, and the slide number as the footer on all slides, except the title slide.

c. Decide on a presentation subject, then think about what results you want to see and what information you will need to create the slide presentation.

d. Insert one picture (your own or one from the Clip Organizer) on each slide, run the available macro for each picture, then move the picture to the center of the slide.

e. Insert one or more appropriate sounds from your computer; you can record a sound, or use one from the Clip Organizer.

f. Insert one or more appropriate videos from your computer or the Clip Organizer.

g. Give each slide a title, and add text where appropriate. Create additional slides as necessary.

h. Apply an appropriate design theme.

i. Check the spelling of the presentation, view the final presentation in Slide Show view, save the final version, then submit the presentation to your instructor. See Figure G-21.

j. Close the presentation, then exit PowerPoint.

**FIGURE G-21**

# Visual Workshop

Create a slide that looks like the example in Figure G-22. The SmartArt is created using the Horizontal Bullet List layout with the Cartoon style and the colored Gradient Loop – Accent 1 color. Save the presentation as **PPT G-California**. Add your name as a footer on the slide, save the presentation, then submit the presentation to your instructor.

**FIGURE G-22**

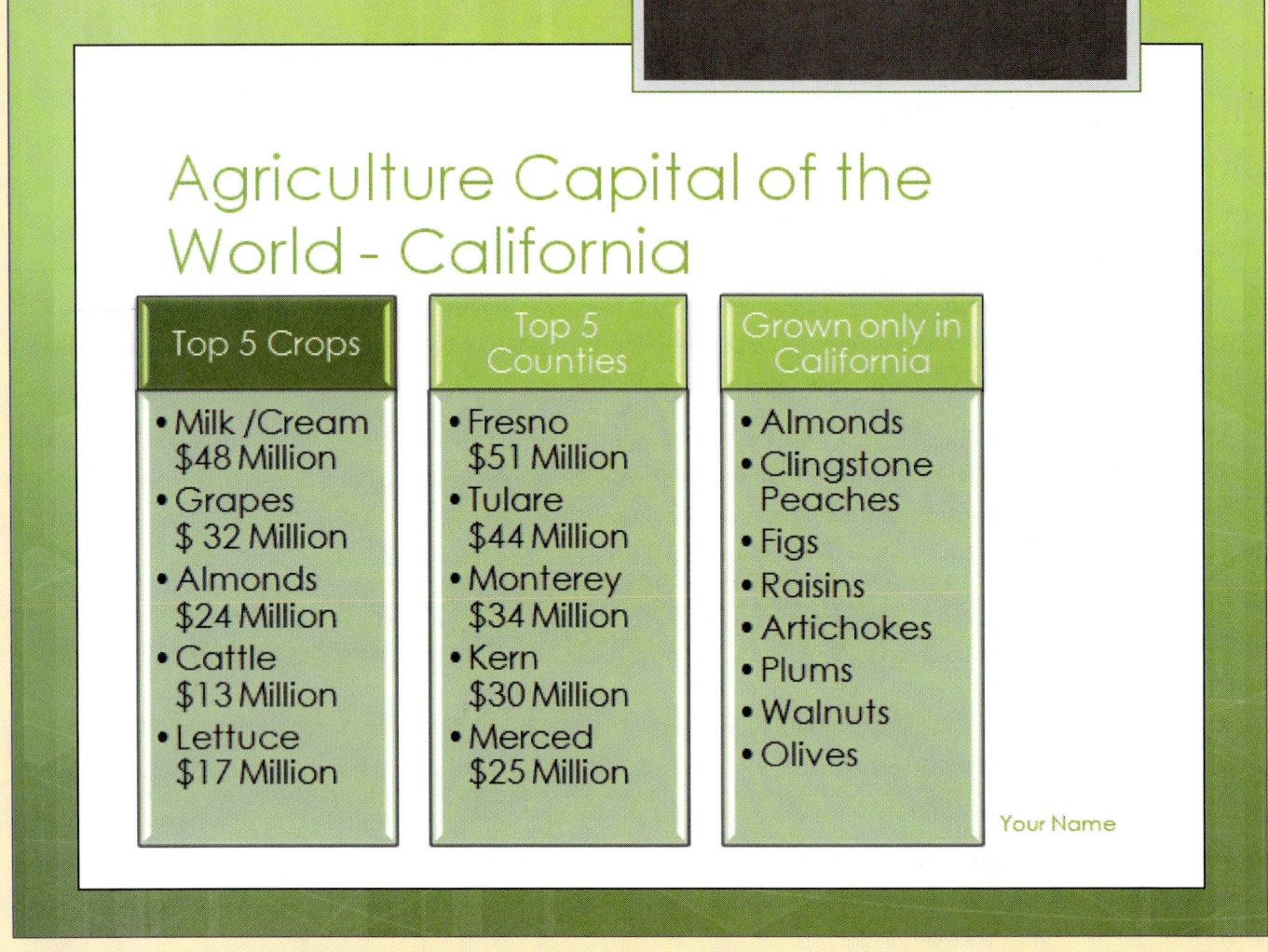

# Using Advanced Features

After your work on a presentation is complete, PowerPoint provides you with several options for preparing and distributing your final presentation. For example, you can send the presentation out for review and receive comments and changes, which you then incorporate into your presentation. At this stage in the process, you can also create customized slide shows and use advanced options to set up and deliver a slide show. You also use PowerPoint to create albums to organize and share your photographs. Before you distribute the Canadian train tour presentation, you need to have other people in the company review it. Once others have reviewed your presentation, you can incorporate their changes and comments. You then create a custom slide show, change slide show options, and prepare the presentation for distribution. You end your day by creating a photo album of your relatives that have worked in the railroad industry and learning about broadcasting a presentation on the Internet.

**OBJECTIVES**

Send a presentation for review

Combine reviewed presentations

Set up a slide show

Create a custom show

Prepare a presentation for distribution

Use templates and add comments

Create a photo album

Broadcast a presentation

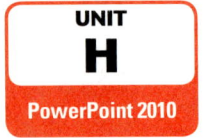

# Sending a Presentation for Review

When you finish creating a presentation, it is often helpful to have others look over the slides for accuracy and clarity. If you are not in the same location as the reviewers, and you have Microsoft Outlook on your computer, you can open Outlook directly from PowerPoint and send a presentation file as an attachment in an e-mail. A reviewer can open the presentation on their computer, make changes and comments, and then e-mail it back to you. Use Outlook to send the presentation to your supervisor for her comments and suggestions.

## STEPS

**TROUBLE**
If you do not have Outlook installed, you will be unable to complete this lesson, skip to the next lesson.

1. **Start PowerPoint, open the presentation PPT H-1.pptx from the drive and folder where your Data Files are stored, then save it as PPT H-QST**

2. **Click the File tab on the Ribbon, click Save & Send, then click the Send as Attachment button in the Send Using E-mail section**

   Microsoft Outlook opens in a new message window as shown in Figure H-1. The subject text box includes the name of the presentation and the Attached text box shows the presentation is automatically attached to the e-mail.

3. **Click the To button in the Outlook message window**

   The Select Names: Contacts dialog box opens. If you have added Contacts to the address book in Outlook, you can use this dialog box to select e-mail addresses for the people you want to review the presentation.

**QUICK TIP**
You can double-click an e-mail address if it is in your Contacts list.

4. **Click Cancel, then type your e-mail address in the To text box**

   Your e-mail address appears in the To text box in the Outlook window.

5. **Click in the message body, then type Please review and get back to me. Thanks.**

   The e-mail is ready to send. Compare your screen to Figure H-2.

6. **Click the Send button in the Outlook message window**

   Outlook sends the e-mail message with the attached presentation file, and the Outlook message window closes.

**QUICK TIP**
If the presentation you are sending for review includes linked files, you need to attach the linked files to your e-mail message or change the linked files to embedded objects.

7. **Start Outlook, click the Send/Receive tab on the Ribbon, then click the Send/Receive All Folders button in the Send & Receive group**

   You may have to wait a short time before the e-mail message you sent to yourself arrives in the Inbox with the PowerPoint file attachment. If the e-mail message is selected, it appears in the Reading pane.

8. **Click the Outlook Close button** ✕

   Outlook closes and the PowerPoint window appears.

**FIGURE H-1:** Outlook message window

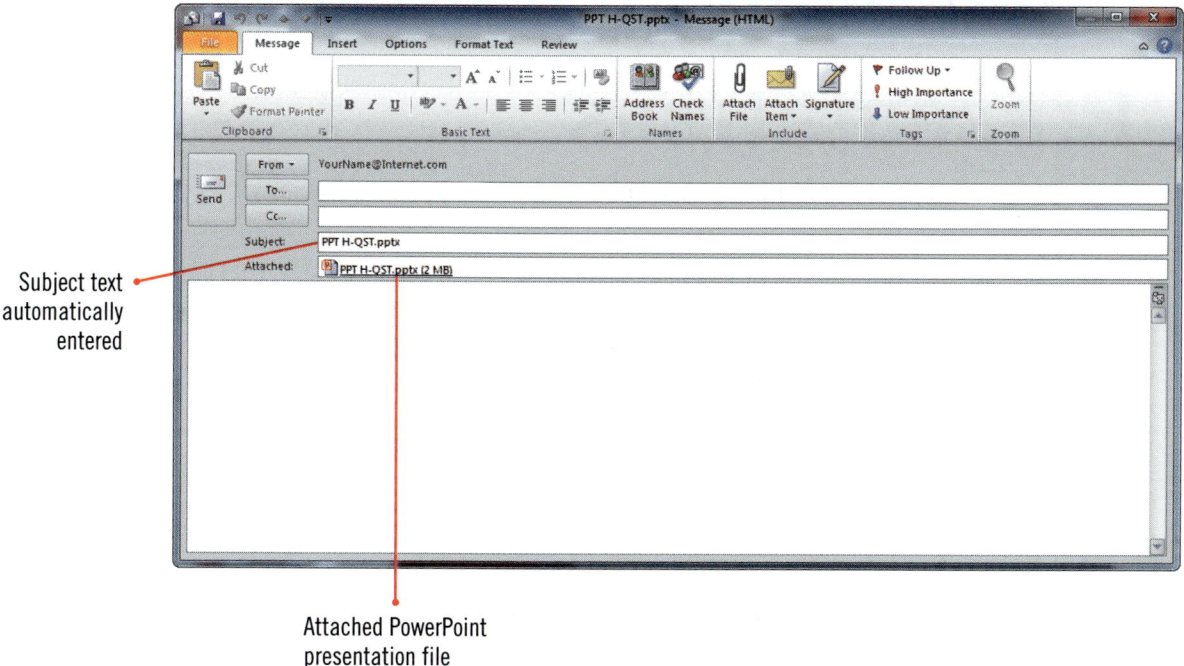

Subject text automatically entered

Attached PowerPoint presentation file

**FIGURE H-2:** Completed Outlook message window

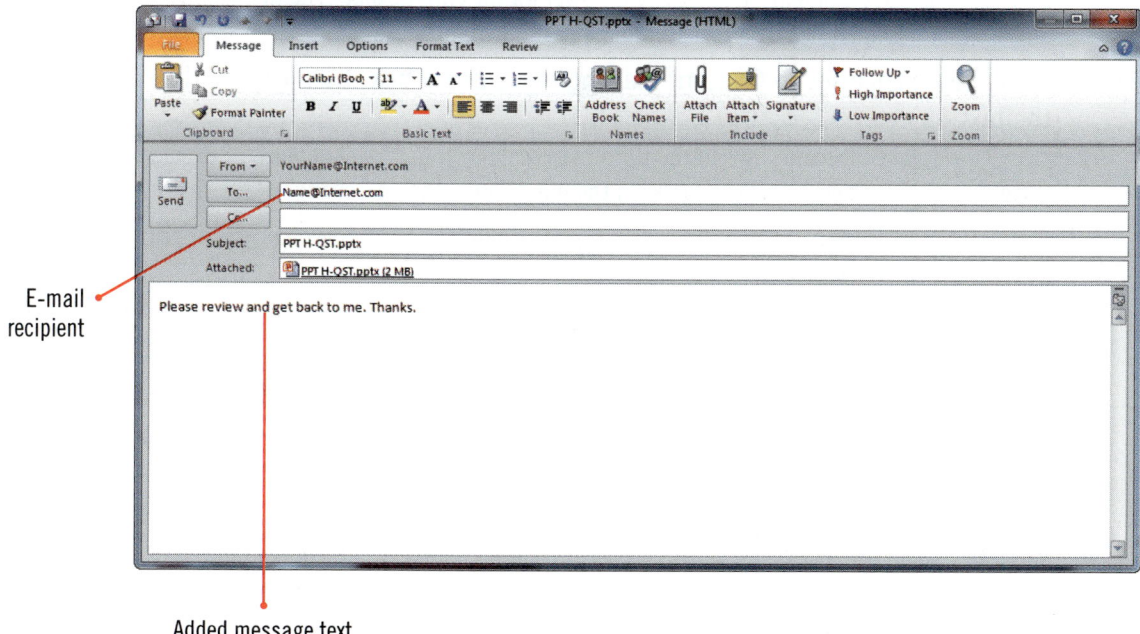

E-mail recipient

Added message text

## Packaging a presentation

Before you copy and distribute one or more presentations, you should always inspect the presentations for personal or confidential information. Once you are ready to save the presentations to a CD or folder, open a presentation, click the File tab, then click Save & Send. Click Package Presentation for CD, then click the Package for CD button. The Package for CD dialog box opens with the current open presentation shown in the list of files to be copied. At this point you can add or remove presentations that you want packaged together. All linked and embedded objects are included in the package. In the Package for CD dialog box, click the Copy to Folder button to save the presentations to a folder on your computer or network, or insert a CD into your computer and click the Copy to CD button. Follow the instructions, then click Close when the saving process is completed.

# Combining Reviewed Presentations

Once a reviewer has completed their review of your presentation and sends it back, you can merge the changes in the reviewer's presentation into your original presentation using the Compare command on the Review tab. You can accept individual changes, changes by slides, changes by reviewer if there is more than one reviewer, or all changes to the presentation. You also have the option or rejecting some or all of the changes. 🎨 You sent the QST presentation to your supervisor who has reviewed the presentation and sent it back to you. You are now ready to combine the reviewed presentation with your original one.

## STEPS

1. **Click the Review tab on the Ribbon, then click the Compare button in the Compare group**
   The Choose File to Merge with Current Presentation dialog box opens.

2. **Locate the presentation PPT H-2.pptx in the drive and folder where you store your Data Files, click PPT H-2.pptx, then click Merge**
   The reviewed presentation is merged with your original one. The Revisions task pane opens on the right side of the screen. It is divided into two tabs: the Slides tab and the Details tab. The Slides tab displays a thumbnail of the current slide and shows what the slide would look like if the suggested changes were made. The Details tab displays individual changes by reviewer for the current slide. The first change is to the text object on Slide 4 and is identified by a reviewer marker as shown in Figure H-3.

**QUICK TIP**
To accept all changes on the current slide or in the whole presentation, click the Accept list arrow, then click the appropriate option.

3. **Click the All changes to Content Placeholder 2 check box, then review the text change in the text object**
   "Easy" replaces "Quick and easy" in the third first-level bullet in the text object. The reviewer marker and all three check boxes now have check marks in them indicating that the change has been accepted.

4. **Click the Next button in the Compare group, click the Review comment thumbnail RBB2 at the top of the slide, then read the comment**
   Slide 9 appears in the Slide pane showing one reviewer marker and one review comment thumbnail labeled RBB2.

5. **Click the Delete button in the Comments group, click the reviewer marker on the slide, then click the Inserted TextBox 2 check box**
   A new formatted text box appears on the slide with information about meals. You decide to reject this change, but will create a slide that discusses meals at a later time.

6. **Click the Inserted TextBox 2 check box to remove the check mark, click the Next button in the Compare group, then click Continue in the message dialog box**
   All of the changes are reviewed. Slide 4 appears in the Slide pane showing the accepted change to the text object.

7. **Click the Next button in the Comments group, then click Continue in message dialog box**
   Slide 1 appears and displays a comment as shown in Figure H-4.

**QUICK TIP**
To reject all changes on the current slide or in the whole presentation, click the Reject list arrow, then click the appropriate option.

8. **Click the Delete list arrow in the Comments group, click Delete All Markup in this Presentation, then click Yes in the message dialog box**
   All of the comments in the presentation are now deleted.

9. **Click the End Review button in the Compare group, read the message dialog box, click Yes, then save your work**
   The Revisions task pane closes.

**FIGURE H-3:** Screen showing open Revisions pane

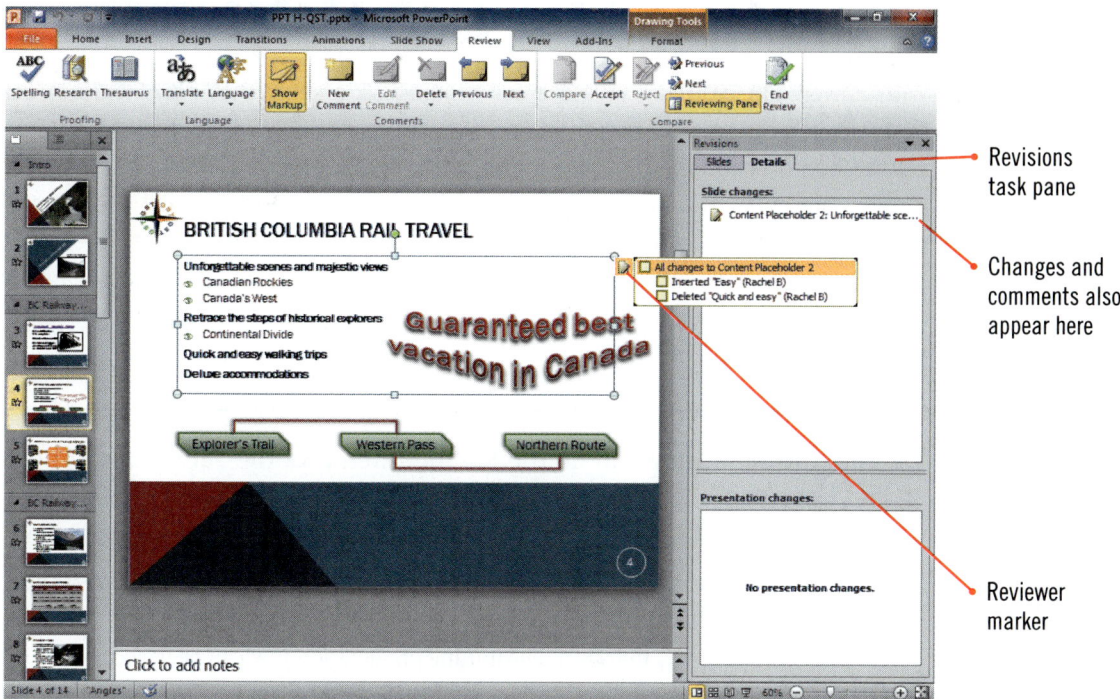

Revisions task pane

Changes and comments also appear here

Reviewer marker

**FIGURE H-4:** Slide with comment

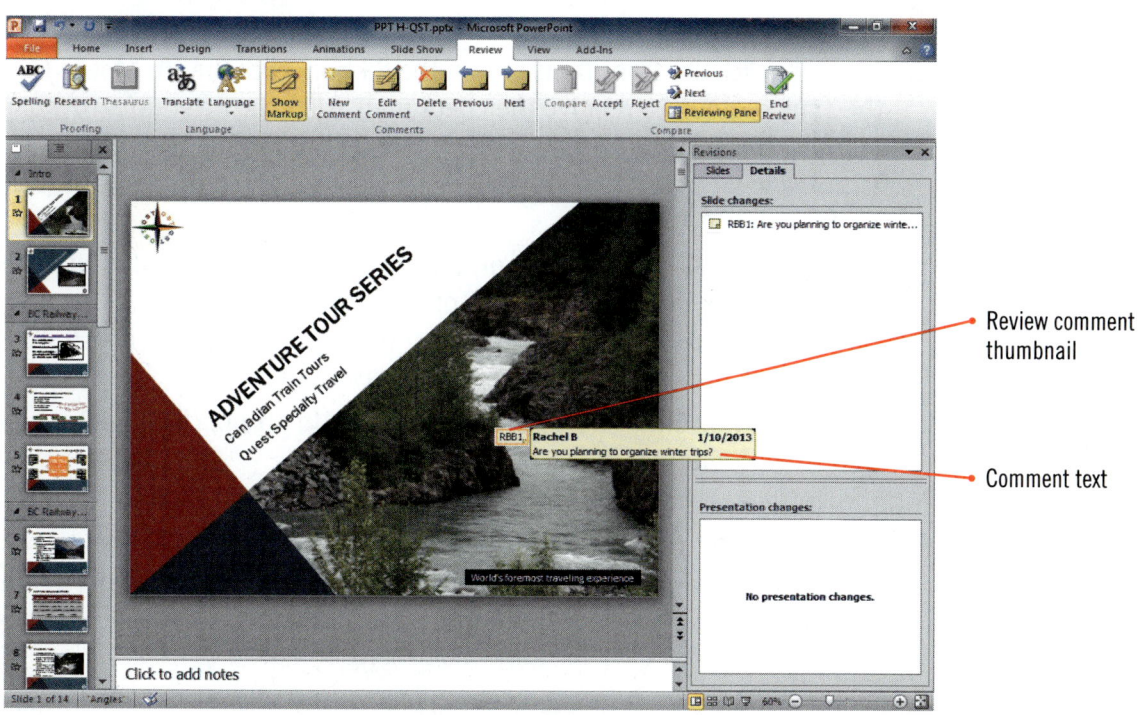

Review comment thumbnail

Comment text

## Coauthoring a presentation

Using collaboration software, such as SharePoint Foundation 2010, Microsoft SharePoint Server 2010, or Microsoft Office Live Workspace, you have the ability to work with others on a presentation over the Internet at the same time. To set up a presentation to be coauthored with you as the original author, click the File tab, click Save & Send, then click Save to SharePoint. Choose a SharePoint location or server to store a primary copy of your presentation, then click the Save As button. All changes made to the presentation are recorded, including who is working on the presentation and where in the presentation they are working. To use this feature, all authors must have PowerPoint 2010 installed on their computers.

PowerPoint 2010

# Setting Up a Slide Show

With PowerPoint, you can create a self-running slide show that plays without user intervention. For example, you can set up a presentation so viewers can watch a slide show on a stand-alone computer, in a small booth or **kiosk**, at a convention, mall, or some other public place. You can also create a self-running presentation on a CD, DVD, or Flash drive for others to watch. You have a number of options when designing a self-running presentation; for example, you can include hyperlinks or action buttons to assist your audience as they move through the presentation. You can also add a synchronized voice that narrates the presentation, and set either manual or automatic slide timings. 🎨 You prepare the presentation so it can be self-running.

## STEPS

1. **Click the Slide Show tab on the Ribbon, then click the Set Up Slide Show button in the Set Up group**

   The Set Up Show dialog box has options you can set to specify how the show will run.

2. **Click the Browsed at a kiosk (full screen) option button in the Show type section of the Set Up Show dialog box**

   This option allows you to have a self-running presentation that can be viewed without a presenter.

3. **Make sure the All option button is selected in the Show slides section, then make sure the Using timings, if present option button is selected in the Advance slides section**

   These settings include all the slides in the presentation and enable PowerPoint to advance the slides at time intervals you set. See Figure H-5.

> **QUICK TIP**
> You must use automatic timings, navigation hyperlinks, or action buttons when you use the kiosk option; otherwise, you will not be able to progress through the slides.

4. **Click OK, click the Transitions tab on the Ribbon, click the On Mouse Click check box in the Timing group to remove the check mark, click the After up arrow until 00:10.00 appears, then click the Apply To All button in the Timing group**

   Each slide in the presentation now will now be displayed for 10 seconds before the slide show advances automatically to the next slide.

5. **Click the Slide Show button 🖵 on the status bar, view the show, let it start again, press [Esc], then click the Slide Show tab on the Ribbon**

   PowerPoint advances the slides automatically at 10-second intervals. After the last slide, the slide show starts over because the kiosk slide show option loops the presentation until someone presses [Esc].

6. **Click the Set Up Slide Show button in the Set Up group, click the Presented by a speaker (full screen) option button, then click OK**

   The slide show options are back to their default settings.

> **QUICK TIP**
> To view a hidden slide while in Slide Show view, right-click the current slide, click Go to Slide, then click the hidden slide.

7. **Click the Slide 1 thumbnail in the Slides tab, click the Hide Slide button in the Set Up group, click the From Beginning button in the Start Slide Show group, then press [Esc]**

   The slide show begins with Slide 2. Notice that Slide 1 in the Slides tab is dimmed and has a hidden slide icon on its number indicating it is hidden, as shown in Figure H-6.

8. **Right-click the Slide 1 thumbnail in the Slides tab, click Hide Slide in the shortcut menu, then save your changes**

   Slide 1 is no longer hidden, or dimmed, and the hidden slide icon is removed.

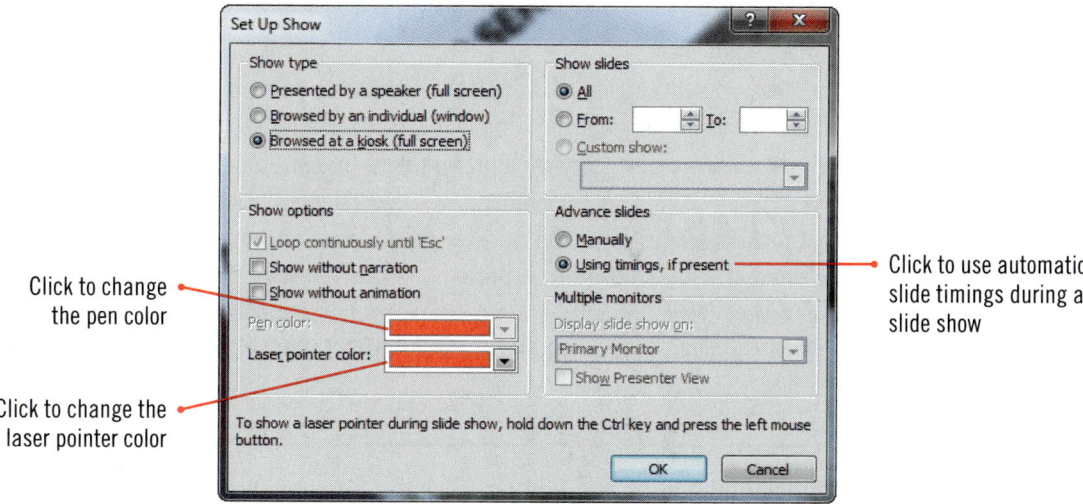

Click to change the pen color

Click to change the laser pointer color

Click to use automatic slide timings during a slide show

FIGURE H-6: Slide 1 is a hidden slide

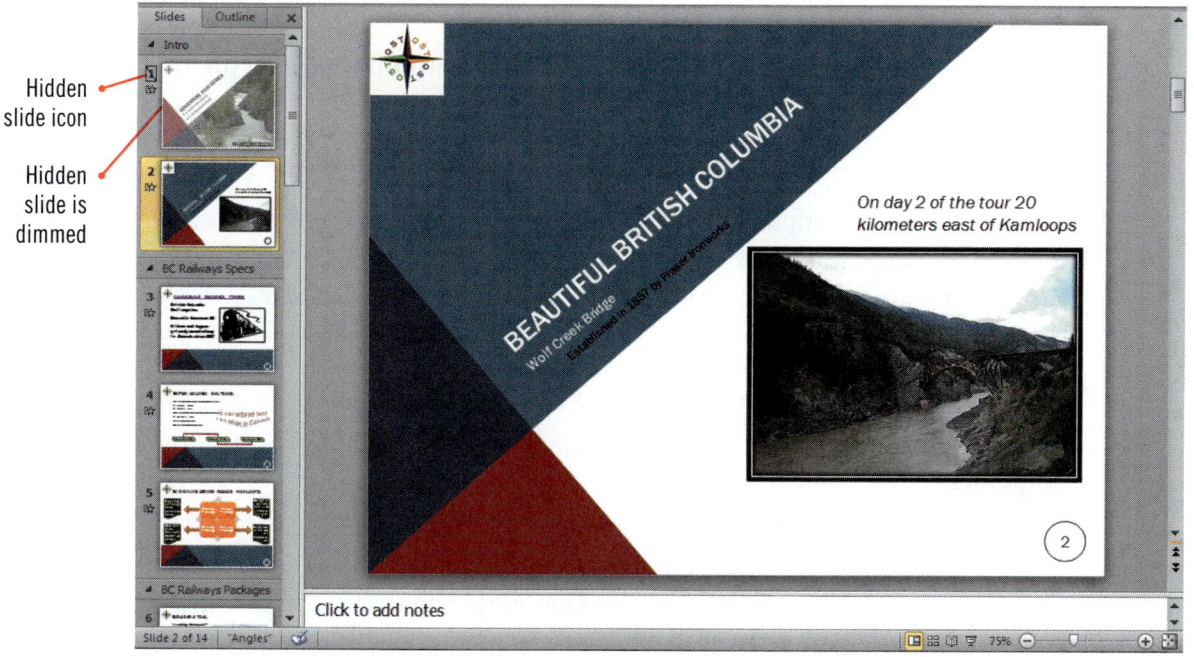

Hidden slide icon

Hidden slide is dimmed

## Using Presenter view

Presenter view is a special PowerPoint view that permits you to run a presentation through two monitors; one monitor that you see on your computer and a second monitor that your audience views. Running a presentation through two monitors provides you more control over your presentation, allowing you to click thumbnails of slides to jump to specific slides and run other programs, if necessary. Presenter view is designed with large icons, buttons, and other tools, which help you easily navigate through a presentation. Speaker notes, not visible to the audience, are easy to read for the presenter. To use this feature, your computer must have multiple monitor capacity, and you need to turn on multiple monitor support and Presenter view. To turn on multiple monitor support, click the Use Presenter View check box in the Monitors group on the Slide Show tab and follow the instructions.

# Creating a Custom Show

A custom show gives you the ability to adapt a presentation for use in different circumstances or with different audiences. For example, you might have a 25-slide presentation that you show to new customers, but only 12 of those slides are necessary for a presentation for existing customers. PowerPoint provides two types of custom shows: basic and hyperlinked. A basic custom show is a separate presentation or a presentation that includes slides from the original presentation. A hyperlinked custom show is a separate (secondary) presentation that is linked to a primary custom show or presentation. 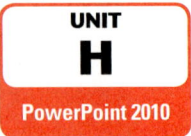 You have been asked to create a version of the Canadian Train Tours presentation for a staff meeting, so you create and view a custom slide show containing only the slides appropriate for that audience. You also learn to use the laser pointer during a slide show.

## STEPS

> **QUICK TIP**
> To print a custom show, click the File tab, click Print, click Print All Slides under Settings, then click the name of the custom show under Custom Shows.

1. **Click the Slide Show tab on the Ribbon, click the Custom Slide Show button in the Start Slide Show group, click Custom Shows to open the Custom Shows dialog box, then click New**

   The Define Custom Show dialog box opens. The slides that are in your current presentation are listed in the Slides in presentation list box.

2. **Press and hold [Ctrl], click Slide 1, click Slides 3–12, release [Ctrl], then click Add**

   The 11 slides you selected move to the Slides in custom show list box, indicating that they will be included in the new presentation. See Figure H-7.

3. **Click 3. British Columbia Rail Travel in the Slides in custom show list, then click the Slide Order up arrow button 🔼 once**

   The slide moves from third place to second place in the list. You can arrange the slides in any order in your custom show by clicking the Slide order up and down arrows.

4. **Click 11. Vacation Comparison Survey, click Remove, drag to select the existing text in the Slide show name text box, type Brief Train Presentation, then click OK**

   The Custom Shows dialog box lists your custom presentation. The custom show is not saved as a separate presentation file on your computer even though you assigned it a new name. To view a custom slide show, you must first open the presentation you used to create the custom show in Slide Show view. You then can open the custom show from the Custom Shows dialog box.

5. **Click Show, view the Brief Train Presentation slide show, then press [Esc] to end the slide show**

   The slides in the custom show appear in the order you set in the Define Custom Show dialog box. At the end of the slide show, you return to the presentation in Normal view.

6. **Click the From Beginning button in the Start Slide Show group, right-click the screen, point to Custom Show, then click Brief Train Presentation**

   The Brief Presentation custom show appears in Slide Show view.

> **QUICK TIP**
> To change the color of the laser pointer, click the Slide Show tab, click the Set Up Slide Show button, then click the Laser pointer color list arrow.

7. **When Slide 3 appears, press and hold [Ctrl], press and hold the left mouse button, move the laser pointer around the slide as shown in Figure H-8, release [Ctrl], release the mouse button, then view the presentation**

   You can use the laser pointer in any presentation on any slide during a slide show.

8. **Press [Esc] at any point to end the slide show, then save your changes**

Using Advanced Features

**FIGURE H-7:** Define Custom Show dialog box

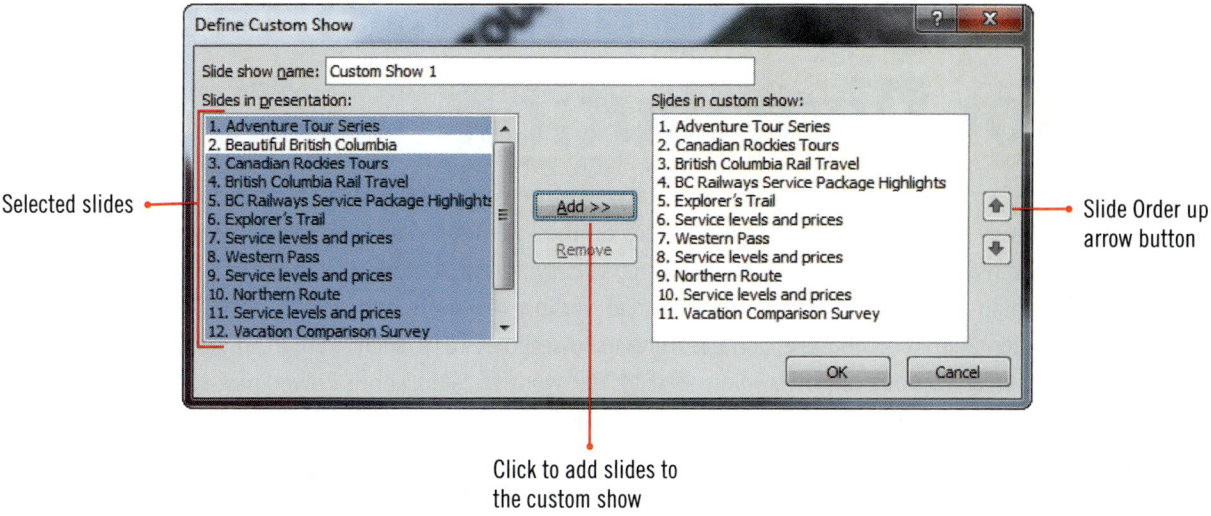

Selected slides

Click to add slides to the custom show

Slide Order up arrow button

**FIGURE H-8:** Screen showing slide 3 in the custom slide show

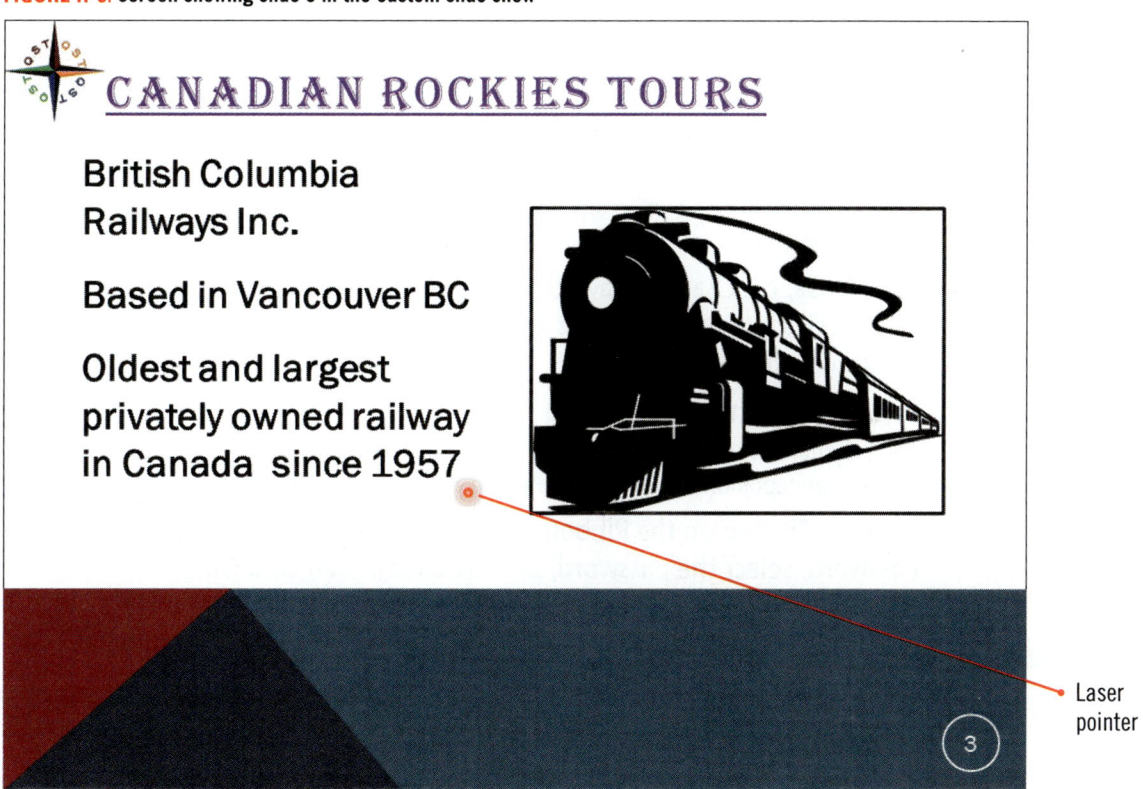

Laser pointer

## Link to a custom slide show

You can use action buttons to switch from the "parent" show to the custom show. Click the Shapes button in the Drawing group on the Home tab, then click an action button. Draw an action button on the slide. Click the Hyperlink to list arrow, click Custom Show, click the custom show you want to link, then click OK. Now when you run a slide show you can click the action button you created to run the custom show. You can also create an interactive table of contents using custom shows. Create your table of contents entries on a slide, then hyperlink each entry to the section it refers to using a custom show for each section.

# Preparing a Presentation for Distribution

Reviewing and preparing your presentation before you share it with others is an essential step, especially with so many security and privacy issues on the Internet today. One way to help secure your PowerPoint presentation is to set a security password, so only authorized people can view or modify its content. If you plan to open a presentation in an earlier version of PowerPoint, it is a good idea to determine if the presentation is compatible. Some features in PowerPoint 2010, such as SmartArt graphics, are not compatible in earlier versions of PowerPoint. 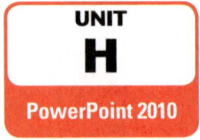 You want to learn about PowerPoint security and compatibility features so you can use them on presentations and other documents.

1.  **Click the Slide 1 thumbnail in the Slides tab, click the File tab on the Ribbon, click the Protect Presentation button, then click Encrypt with Password**
    The Encrypt Document dialog box opens.

2.  **Type 123abc**
    As you type the password, solid black symbols appear in the text box, which makes it unreadable, as shown in Figure H-9. If anyone is looking at your screen while you type, this helps protect the confidentiality of your password.

    **TROUBLE**
    If you mistype the password in the Confirm Password dialog box, an alert dialog box opens.

3.  **Click OK to open the Confirm Password dialog box, type 123abc, then click OK**
    The presentation is now set with a password. Once the presentation is closed, this password must be entered in a Password dialog box to open the presentation. The presentation is **encrypted**, protected from unauthorized users.

4.  **Click Close, click Save to save changes, click the File tab, click Recent, then click PPT H-QST.pptx on the Recent Presentations list to open the file**
    The Password dialog box opens.

    **QUICK TIP**
    To set other password options, open the Save As dialog box, click Tools, then click General Options.

5.  **Type 123abc, then click OK**
    The presentation opens. Be aware that if you don't remember your password, there is no way to retrieve it from the presentation or from Microsoft, and you will not be able to open or view your presentation.

6.  **Click the File tab on the Ribbon, click the Protect Presentation button, click Encrypt with Password, select the password, press [Delete], then click OK**
    The password is removed and is no longer needed to open the presentation.

    **QUICK TIP**
    The Check Accessibility feature checks for potential issues that might be difficult for people with disabilities to read. Click the File tab, click the Check for Issues button, then click Check Accessibility to open the Accessibility Checker task pane.

7.  **Click the Check for Issues button, then click Check Compatibility**
    The Compatibility Checker analyzes the presentation, then the Microsoft PowerPoint Compatibility Checker dialog box opens, as shown in Figure H-10. Each item in the dialog box represents a feature that is not supported in earlier versions of PowerPoint. This means that if you try to run this presentation using an earlier version of PowerPoint, the items listed will function in a limited capacity or not at all.

8.  **Click the down scroll arrow, read all of the items in the dialog box, click OK, add your name to the notes and handouts footer, then click the Slide Sorter button 🔲 on the status bar**
    The dialog box closes. Compare your screen to Figure H-11.

9.  **Save your work, submit your presentation to your instructor, then close the presentation but do not exit PowerPoint**

**FIGURE H-9:** Encrypt Document dialog box

Encrypted password

**FIGURE H-10:** Compatibility Checker dialog box

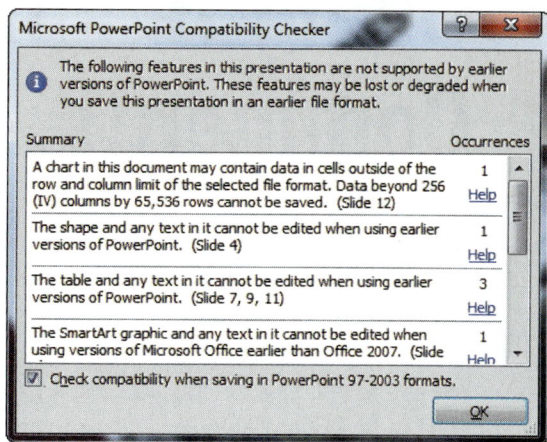

**FIGURE H-11:** Final presentation in Slide Sorter view

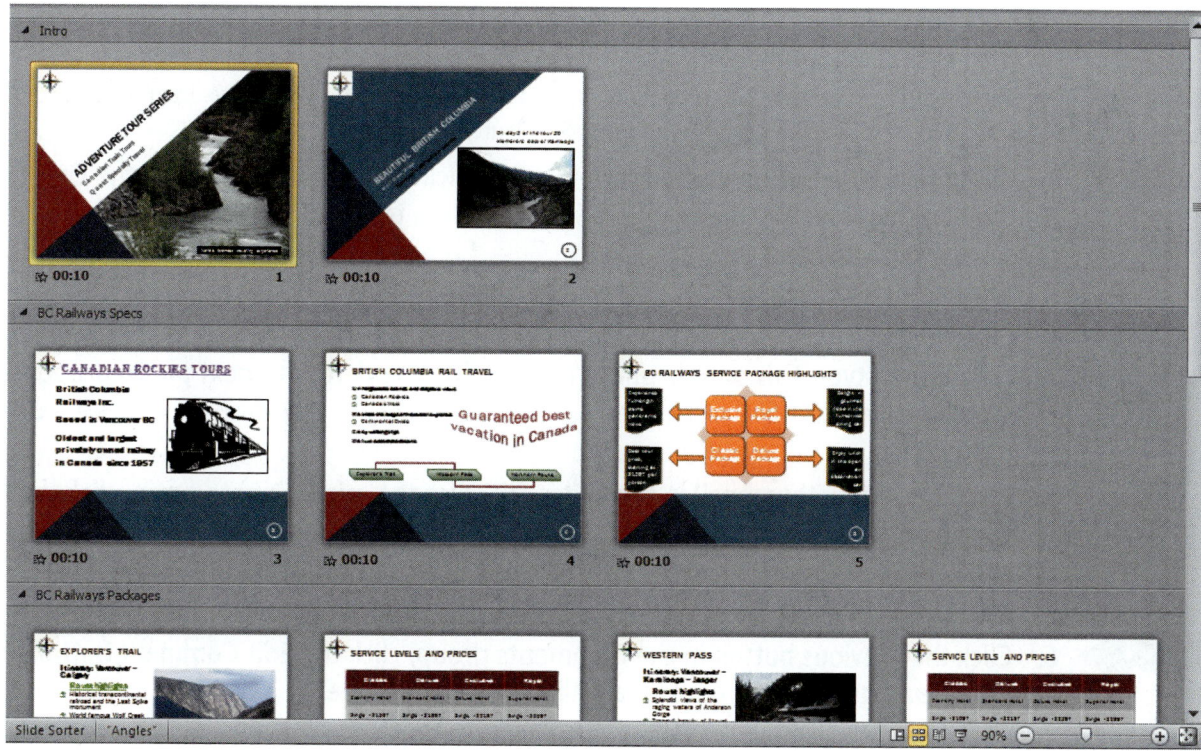

## Creating a strong password

Creating a strong password is a vital part of securing your presentations, other sensitive documents, Internet accounts, and personal information. The strongest password is a random complex string of lowercase and uppercase characters and numbers. For example, the password used in this lesson, 123abc, is a weak password. Though it has both numbers and lowercase letters, it is an easy sequential password that someone could guess. Here are

some simple guidelines to making a good password: (1) make the password long by using eight or more characters; (2) use a variety of uppercase and lowercase letters, symbols, and numbers; (3) if possible use words or phrases that you can remember that are difficult for others to guess; (4) keep your password secret and never reveal it in an e-mail; and (5) regularly change your password.

# Using Templates and Adding Comments

PowerPoint offers you a variety of ways to create a presentation including beginning with a blank presentation, a theme, a template, or an existing presentation. A **template** is a type of presentation that contains custom design information made to the slide master and slide layouts. A template can contain theme colors, theme fonts, theme effects, background styles, and even content. PowerPoint installs a number of templates on your computer that include the standard Blank presentation and Sample templates. You also have access to templates online from the Office.com Web site that you can download.  You need to review available PowerPoint templates that could be used to display pictures of upcoming tour specials for the company Web site.

**STEPS**

1. **Click the File tab on the Ribbon, then click New**

   The Available Templates and Themes pane opens in Backstage view. Blank Presentation is selected.

2. **Click Sample templates, click each template thumbnail to view it in the Preview pane, then click Contemporary Photo Album**

   These templates are installed on your computer and are available for you to use. Each template comes with sample content including graphics and text. See Figure H-12.

3. **Click the Create button in the Preview pane, click the Save button 🖫 on the Quick Access toolbar, then save the file as PPT H-Sample Album to the drive and folder where you store your Data Files**

   A new presentation with six slides appears in the program window.

**QUICK TIP**

You can copy the text of a comment to the slide by clicking the review comment thumbnail, then dragging the comment text to a blank area on the slide.

4. **Click the Review tab on the Ribbon, click the New Comment button in the Comments group, then type This sample photo album might work for our next photo proposal.**

   A new comment text box appears next to the review comment thumbnail on the slide, as shown in Figure H-13.

5. **Click the Slide 5 thumbnail in the Slides tab, click the middle photograph, click the New Comment button in the Comments group, then type The use of different picture styles looks great.**

   A new comment appears on Slide 5 next to the middle photograph.

**QUICK TIP**

Double-click the review comment thumbnail to open the comment text box to add to or edit the comment text.

6. **Click the Previous button in the Comments group, click the Edit Comment button in the Comments group, then type I really like this picture style.**

   The comment text box opens. To add or edit comment text, you need to open the comment text box.

7. **Click the Show Markup button in the Comments group**

   The review comment thumbnail and comment text box on Slide 1 are hidden. The Show Markup button is a toggle button, which alternates between showing and hiding comments.

8. **Click the Next button in the Comments group, then click the Show Markup button in the Comments group, add your name to the slide footer, then save your work**

   The review comment thumbnail is visible again. After you save the presentation, the review comment thumbnail changes to A2 identifying the comment as the second comment made by the author of the presentation.

9. **Submit your presentation to your instructor, then close the presentation but do not exit PowerPoint**

**FIGURE H-12:** Screen showing sample templates

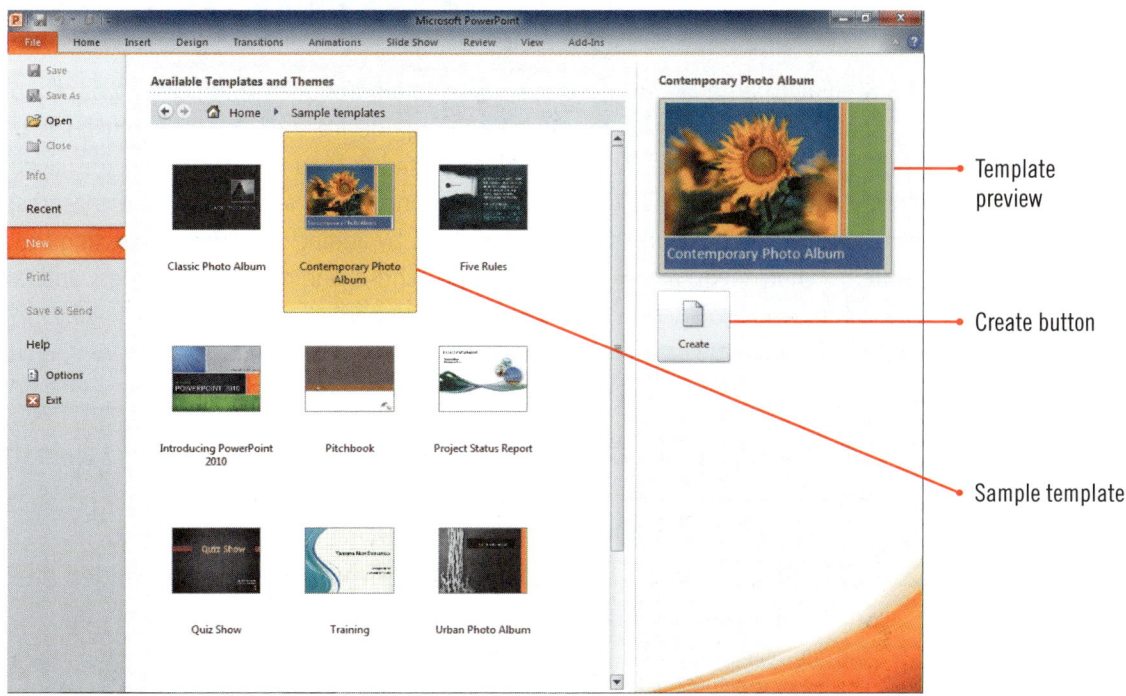

Template preview

Create button

Sample template

**FIGURE H-13:** Slide showing applied template and new comment

Review comment thumbnail

New template with sample content appears on six slides

Today's date appears here

New comment

Comment text box

## Saving a presentation to SkyDrive on Windows Live

SkyDrive is a free password-protected online storage service provided by Microsoft at the Windows Live Web site on the Internet. Files you upload and store on SkyDrive can be opened from any computer in the world that has access to the Internet. You can store up to 25 GB on SkyDrive, and you have the capability of sharing files with others you are connected with on your Windows Live network. To take advantage of this service you need to first have a Windows Live ID, which you can get from the Windows Live Web site. Then, to save a presentation file to SkyDrive, click the File tab on the Ribbon, click Save & Send, click Save to Web, click the Sign In button, then follow the directions.

# Creating a Photo Album

A PowerPoint photo album is a special presentation designed specifically to display photographs. You can add pictures to a photo album from any storage device such as a hard drive, flash drive, digital camera, scanner, or Web camera. As with any presentation, you can customize the layout of a photo album presentation by adding title text to slides, applying frames around the pictures, and applying a theme. You can also format the pictures of the photo album by adding a caption, converting the pictures to black and white, rotating them, applying artistic effects, and changing their brightness and contrast.  On a break from work, you decide to create a personal photo album showing some of your relatives who worked for the railroad in the early and mid-20th century.

1. **Click the Insert tab on the Ribbon, click the Photo Album list arrow in the Images group, then click New Photo Album**

   The Photo Album dialog box opens.

2. **Click File/Disk, select the file PPT H-3.jpg from the drive and folder where you store your Data Files, then click Insert**

   The photograph appears in the Preview box and is listed in the Pictures in album list, as shown in Figure H-14. The buttons below the Preview box allow you to rotate the photo or change its contrast or brightness.

3. **Click File/Disk, click the file PPT H-4.jpg, press and hold [Shift], click the file PPT H-7.jpg, release [Shift], then click Insert**

   Four more photographs appear in the dialog box.

4. **Click Create, save the presentation as PPT H-Photo Album to the drive and folder where you store your Data Files, then change the slide title to Family Railroad Engineers**

   A new presentation opens. PowerPoint creates a title slide along with a slide for each photograph that you inserted. The computer user name appears in the subtitle text box by default.

5. **Click the Photo Album list arrow in the Images group, then click Edit Photo Album**

   The Edit Photo Album dialog box opens. You can use this dialog box to format the photographs and slide layout of your photo album presentation.

6. **Click PPT H-3.jpg in the Pictures in album list, press and hold [Shift], click PPT H-7.jpg, release [Shift], click the Picture layout list arrow in the Album Layout section, click 1 picture with title, click the Frame shape list arrow, click Center Shadow Rectangle, then click Update**

   All of the slides now have a title text placeholder, and the photographs are formatted with a shadow and centered on each slide.

7. **Referring to Figure H-15, click each slide thumbnail in the Slides pane, add the corresponding title to each slide, then click the Slide Sorter view button 🔲 on the status bar**

   All of the slides now have a title.

8. **Drag the Zoom Slider ▽ on the status bar until your screen looks similar to Figure H-15, then add your name to the slides footer**

9. **Save your changes, submit your presentation to your instructor, close the presentation, then exit PowerPoint**

**FIGURE H-14:** Photo Album dialog box

File/Disk button

Up and Down buttons

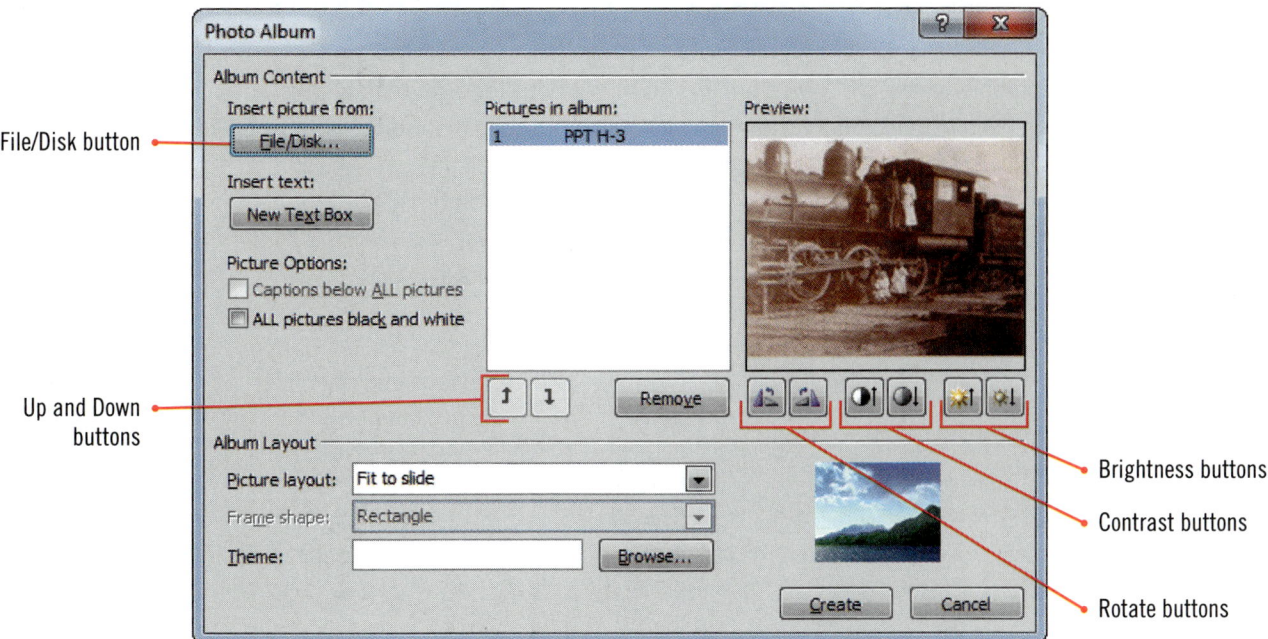

Brightness buttons

Contrast buttons

Rotate buttons

**FIGURE H-15:** Completed photo album

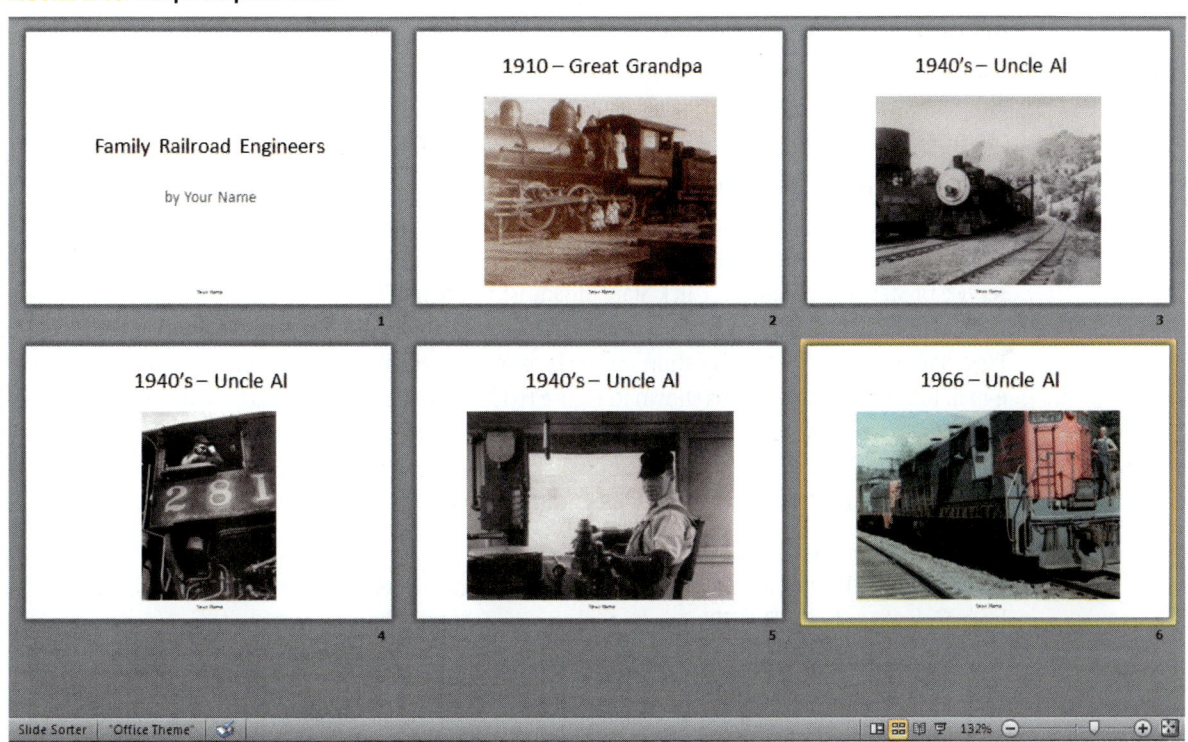

## Recording a slide show

With the Record Slide Show feature you have the ability to record and save audio narrations, slide and animation timings, and laser pointer gestures for each slide during a slide show. This feature is great to use if you want to record audience comments so that people who were unable to attend the presentation live can view and listen to it later. To record a slide show, click the Slide Show tab, click the Record Slide Show list arrow in the Set Up group, then start the recording from the beginning of the current slide. You then have to choose which elements you want to record during the slide show. If you choose to record audio narrations, you must have a microphone, a sound card, and speakers. A sound icon appears on every narrated slide.

# Broadcasting a Presentation

Being able to assemble everyone in the same room for a presentation can be difficult, which is why the PowerPoint broadcasting feature provides a way to share your presentation to a remote audience. You can use PowerPoint to broadcast a presentation to an audience over the Internet in real time using a Web browser.  In preparation for hosting a presentation broadcast to others in your company, you learn the basics of broadcasting from PowerPoint.

**DETAILS**

**QUICK TIP**

Be careful. Anyone with access to the broadcast service and the URL link to your slide show can view the presentation.

- ### Broadcast overview

  Using the Broadcast Slide Show feature in PowerPoint, you can present a slide show to anyone on the Internet. To view the presentation broadcast, audience members need to have an Internet address (URL) link so they can access your broadcast on the Internet. You can e-mail your audience members the URL for your slide show before or during the broadcast without interfering with the broadcast. You are required to have a network service to host a broadcast, like the PowerPoint Broadcast Service, which is available to anyone on the Internet with a Windows Live ID. You can also use a broadcast service provided by your company or organization that has Microsoft Office Web Apps installed.

- ### Prepare a presentation for a broadcast

  Before you attempt to broadcast a presentation slide show, make sure you are connected to the Internet or an organization server with a broadcast site and Office Web Apps installed. To host a broadcast, you need to use one of the supported Web browsers: Internet Explorer, Firefox, or Safari. Not all PowerPoint features are supported for broadcasting, and some features are altered. For example, slide transitions in your presentation are converted to Fade and sounds, including narrations, or videos are not transmitted. Also, you cannot annotate or markup slides during a broadcast, and hyperlinks are not shown to your audience. Keep in mind too that the broadcast service you use might impose file size limitations on broadcasted presentation files.

- ### Broadcast a presentation

  To broadcast a presentation, click the Broadcast Slide Show button in the Start Slide Show group on the Slide Show tab. The Broadcast Slide Show dialog box opens as shown in Figure H-16. You can change the broadcast service or start the broadcast. Click Start Broadcast to open a Windows Security dialog box, where you enter your user name and password to access the broadcast site. After you enter your user name and password, PowerPoint sets up the URL location on the broadcast server and displays the URL link that you can copy or e-mail to audience members as shown in Figure H-17. A Broadcast View message bar appears below the Ribbon in the PowerPoint window and alerts you that you are currently broadcasting and cannot make any changes to the presentation. Click Start Slide Show in the dialog box to open the presentation in Slide Show view. Click the End Broadcast button in the Broadcast group to end the broadcast.

- ### View a presentation broadcast

  To view a broadcast as an audience member, you need to open the Internet address (URL) provided by the host of the broadcast. The URL can be sent to audience members in an e-mail or copied and sent. When an audience member clicks the slide show URL link, the slide show opens in their Web browser. The audience follows along live as you present the slide show broadcast.

**FIGURE H-16:** Broadcast Slide Show dialog box

Current broadcast service

Click to change broadcast services

**FIGURE H-17:** Screen showing presentation broadcast

Broadcast tab commands

Broadcast View message bar

URL link

Click to send the URL link using e-mail

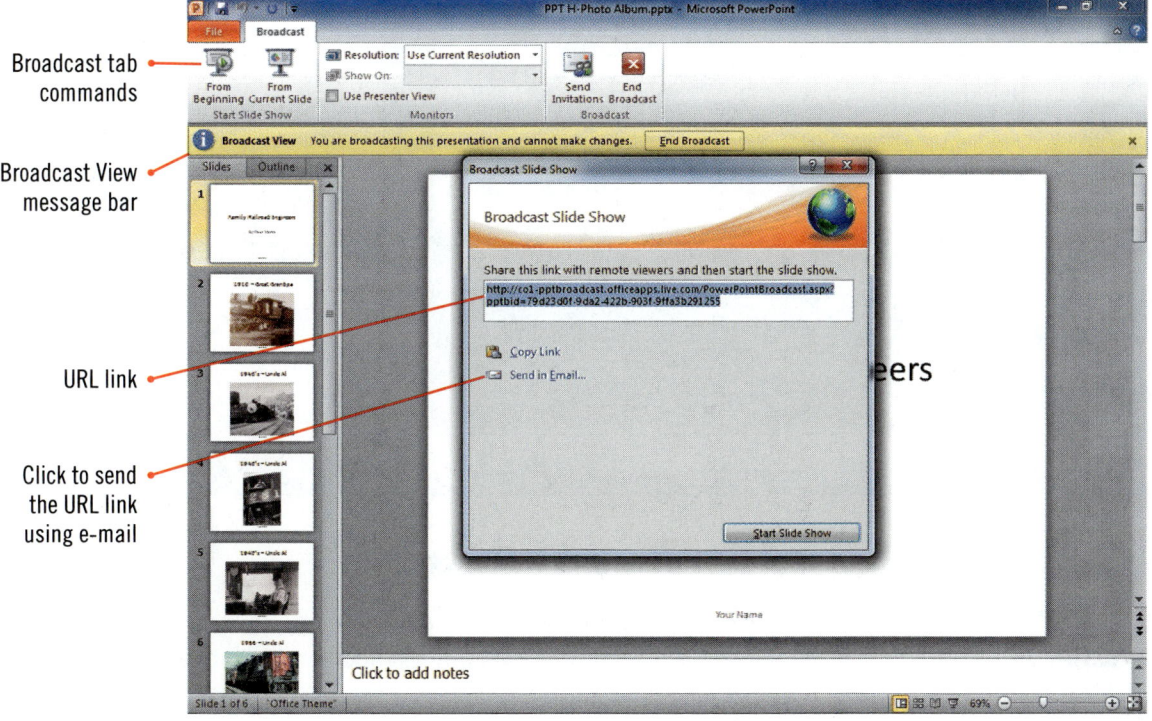

PowerPoint 2010

## Publish slides to a Slide Library

If your computer is connected to a network server running Office SharePoint Server 2007 or Office SharePoint Server 2010 software, you can store slides in a folder called a **Slide Library** for others to access, modify, and use. Using a Slide Library, others can make changes to your slides, and you in turn can track and review all changes and have access to the latest version of your slides. To publish slides from PowerPoint to a Slide Library (after a Slide Library is created on a server), click the File tab, click Save & Send, click Publish Slides, then click the Publish Slides button. The Publish Slides dialog box opens. Use Browse in the dialog box to select the Slide Library location you are going to use. To add slides to a Slide Library, click the check box next to each slide, then click Publish.

# Practice

## Concepts Review

For current SAM information, including versions and content details, visit SAM Central (http://www.cengage.com/samcentral). If you have a SAM user profile, you may have access to hands-on instruction, practice, and assessment of the skills covered in this unit. Since various versions of SAM are supported throughout the life of this text, check with your instructor for the correct instructions and URL/Web site for accessing assignments.

## Label each element of the PowerPoint window shown in Figure H-18.

**FIGURE H-18**

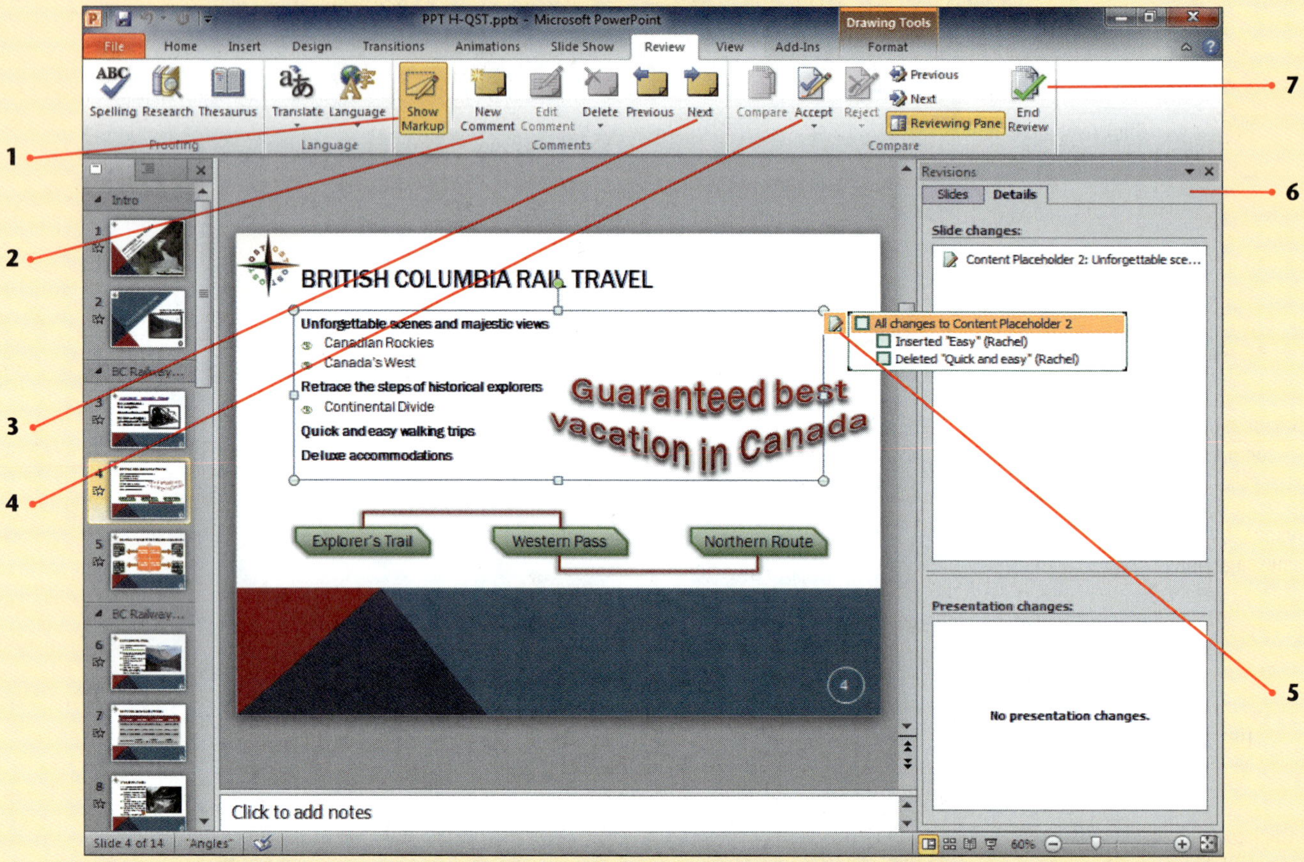

## Match each term with the statement that best describes its function.

**8. Slide Library**

**9. Hyperlinked custom show**

**10. Basic custom show**

**11. Kiosk**

**12. Template**

**a.** A separate presentation that is connected to a custom show

**b.** A folder on a network server that stores slides for others to access and modify

**c.** A special slide show created from selected slides in a presentation

**d.** A small booth for a stand-alone computer that can run a slide show without user intervention

**e.** A type of presentation that contains custom design and content

**Select the best answer from the list of choices.**

13. When you combine two presentations together, you are _____ all the changes from one presentation into your original presentation.
    - **a.** linking
    - **b.** merging
    - **c.** removing
    - **d.** hyperlinking

14. Which view allows you to view a presentation using two monitors?
    - **a.** Multiple Monitor view
    - **b.** Reading view
    - **c.** Presenter view
    - **d.** Theater view

15. Which of the following statements is *not* true about a presentation set to run at a stand-alone computer?
    - **a.** You don't have to be present to run the slide show.
    - **b.** You can use action buttons to progress through the slides.
    - **c.** The presentation can loop continuously.
    - **d.** The presentation works best with manual slide timings.

16. What do you create when you want to show specific slides in a presentation to a specific audience?
    - **a.** Encrypted file
    - **b.** Broadcast
    - **c.** Template
    - **d.** Custom show

17. Creating a _____ helps keep your presentation secure.
    - **a.** password
    - **b.** hyperlink
    - **c.** shared server
    - **d.** Slide Library

18. A _____ is a special presentation designed specifically to display pictures.
    - **a.** broadcast
    - **b.** picture template
    - **c.** photo album
    - **d.** Slide Library

19. Which of the following identifies features that might not work in earlier versions of PowerPoint?
    - **a.** SkyDrive Server
    - **b.** Compatibility Checker
    - **c.** Kiosk
    - **d.** Document Inspector

20. You can use PowerPoint to _____ a presentation to a remote audience over the Internet.
    - **a.** broadcast
    - **b.** publish
    - **c.** package
    - **d.** review

# Skills Review

1. **Send a presentation for review.**
    - **a.** Start PowerPoint, open the file PPT H-8.pptx from the drive and folder where you store your Data Files, then save it as **PPT H-NY Cafe**. (*Note*: You need to have Outlook set up to complete the next three steps.)
    - **b.** Click the File tab, click Save & Send, then click the Send as Attachment button.
    - **c.** Type a brief message in the e-mail message, then send the presentation to yourself.
    - **d.** Open Microsoft Outlook, open the message you sent to yourself, then close Outlook.

2. **Combine reviewed presentations.**
    - **a.** Click the Review tab, then click the Compare button in the Compare group.
    - **b.** Locate the presentation PPT H-9.pptx from the drive and folder where you store your Data Files, click PPT H-9.pptx, then click Merge.
    - **c.** Read the comment on the slide, delete the comment, then click the check box to accept the changes on Slide 3.
    - **d.** Click the Next button in the Compare group, then click Continue in the message dialog box.
    - **e.** Click the Slide 1 thumbnail in the Slides tab, click the Next button in the Comments group, read the comment on Slide 2, then delete the comment.
    - **f.** End the review, click Yes to save the review changes, then save your work.

## Skills Review (continued)

**3. Set up a slide show.**

   **a.** Click the Slide Show tab, click the Set Up Slide Show button, set up a slide show that will be browsed at a kiosk, using automatic slide timings, then click the Transitions tab.

   **b.** Remove the check mark from the On Mouse Click check box, set a slide timing of 5 seconds to all the slides, run the slide show all the way through once, then press [Esc] to end the slide show.

   **c.** Change the slide show options to run using manual slide timings and presented by a speaker.

   **d.** Run through the slide show from Slide 1 using the action buttons at the bottom of the slides. Move forward and backward through the presentation, watching the animation effects as they appear, then press [Esc] when you are finished.

   **e.** Hide Slide 5, run through the slide show, then unhide Slide 5.

   **f.** When you have finished viewing the slide show, reset the slide timings to automatic, then save your changes.

**4. Create a custom show.**

   **a.** Create a custom show called **Goals** which includes Slides 2, 3, 4, and 5.

   **b.** Move Slide 3 Performance Series above Slide 2 Lecture Series.

   **c.** View the show from within the Custom Shows dialog box, then press [Esc] to end the slide show.

   **d.** Go to Slide 1, begin the slide show, then, when Slide 1 appears, go to the Goals custom show.

   **e.** View the custom slide show, return to Normal view, then save your changes.

**5. Prepare a presentation for distribution.**

   **a.** Click the File tab, click Protect Presentation, then click Encrypt with Password.

   **b.** Type 12345, then type the same password in the Confirm Password dialog box.

   **c.** Close the presentation, save your changes, open the presentation, then type **12345** in the Password dialog box.

   **d.** Open the Encrypt Document dialog box again, then delete the password.

   **e.** Click the File tab, click Check for Issues, click Check Compatibility, read the information, then close the dialog box.

   **f.** Save your work, add your name to the notes and handouts footer, then check the spelling in the presentation. The completed presentation is shown in Figure H-19.

   **g.** Submit your presentation to your instructor, then close the presentation.

**6. Use templates and add comments.**

   **a.** Click the File tab, click New, click Sample templates, click Classic Photo Album, then click Create.

   **b.** Save the presentation as **PPT H-Classic Photo Album** to the drive and folder where you store your Data Files.

   **c.** Click the Review tab on the Ribbon, click the New Comment button, type **What do you think of this design for our new photo series?**, then go to Slide 3.

**FIGURE H-19**

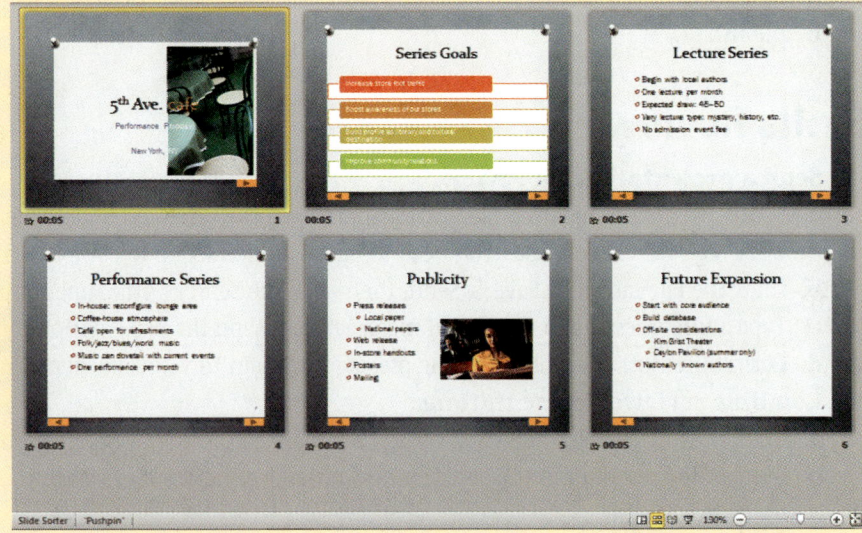

   **d.** Add a new comment, type **This is an interesting photo layout.**, click the Previous button, then click the Edit Comment button.

   **e.** Type **I like this title slide design.**, add your name to the slide footer, then save your work.

   **f.** Submit your presentation to your instructor, then close the presentation.

## Skills Review (continued)

**7. Create a photo album.**

**a.** Create a photo album presentation, then from the drive and folder where you store your Data Files, insert the files PPT H-10.jpg, PPT H-11.jpg, PPT H-12.jpg, PPT H-13.jpg, PPT H-14.jpg, PPT H-15.jpg, PPT H-16.jpg, and PPT H-17.jpg.

**b.** Move picture PPT H-15.jpg so it is second in the list, move PPT H-12.jpg so it is last in the list, create the photo album, then save it as **PPT H-Vacation** to the drive and folder where you store your Data Files.

**c.** Change the title on the title slide to **My Vacation in the West**, then type your name in the subtitle text box.

**d.** Open the Edit Photo Album dialog box, change the picture layout to 1 picture, change the frame shape to Simple Frame, White, then update the presentation.

**FIGURE H-20**

**e.** Apply a solid black background (Design tab) to all the slides, add your name to the slide footer on all slides except the title slide, then save your changes. The completed photo album is shown in Figure H-20.

**f.** Submit your presentation to your instructor, close the presentation, then exit PowerPoint.

# Independent Challenge 1

You work for Island Getaways, Inc., an international tour company that provides specialty tours to destinations throughout Asia and the Pacific. You have to develop presentations that the sales force can use to highlight different tours at conferences and meetings. To complete the presentation, you need to create at least two of your own slides. Assume that Island Getaways has a special (20% off regular price) on tours to Fiji and the Cook Islands during the spring of 2013. Also assume that Island Getaways offers tour packages to the Philippines, Japan, Australia, and New Zealand.

**a.** Start PowerPoint, open the presentation PPT H-18.pptx, then save it as **PPT H-Islands** to the drive and folder where you store your Data Files.

**b.** Open the Review tab on the Ribbon, use the Next button in the Comments group to view each comment, read the comment, then delete the last comment on the Departing Cities slide.

**c.** Use the Previous button in the Comments group to move back to slides that have comments, write a new comment in response to each of the original comments, then move each review comment thumbnail next to the original review comment thumbnails.

**d.** Use the Compatibility Checker on the presentation.

**e.** Use the information provided above to help you develop additional content for two new slides.

**f.** Insert at least three different media clips (pictures, clip art videos, videos, clip art, or sounds). Use clips from PowerPoint or from other approved legal media sources.

**g.** Apply slide transitions, timings, and animations to all the slides in the presentation.

# Independent Challenge 1 (continued)

**h.** Apply a saved design theme. On the Design tab, click the Themes More button, click Browse for Themes, then apply the PPT H-19.thmx theme from the drive and folder where you store your Data Files.

**i.** Convert the text on Slide 2 to a SmartArt diagram, then format the diagram using the techniques you learned in this book.

**j.** Use the Compatibility Checker again on the presentation. Note any differences, then view in Slide Show view.

**k.** Add your name as a footer on all notes and handouts, then check the spelling in the presentation.

**l.** Submit your presentation to your instructor, close the presentation, then exit PowerPoint.

# Independent Challenge 2

You work in Monterey, California, at the State Agricultural Statistics Agency. Part of your job is to compile agricultural information gathered from the counties of California and create presentations that display the data for public viewing. You are currently working on a summary presentation that will be made public on the agency Web site.

**a.** Start PowerPoint, open the presentation PPT H-20.pptx, then save it as **PPT H-Ag Report** to the drive and folder where you store your Data Files.

**b.** Convert the information on Slide 5 to a SmartArt diagram using one of the Picture list layouts. Insert the file PPT H-21.jpg from the drive and folder where you store your Data Files for all of the pictures in the SmartArt graphic.

**c.** Format the SmartArt diagram using the commands on the SmartArt Tools Design and Format tabs.

**d.** Format the table on Slide 4. Change the table layout so the table displays the information properly, split the Cattle and Calves cell into two cells, then format the table.

**e.** Create a custom slide show that displays any four slides from the presentation.

**f.** Insert appropriate media clips on at least two slides.

**Advanced Challenge Exercise** *(requires Internet connection and instructor approval)*

- Write at least two comments in the presentation, then send the presentation as an e-mail attachment to another student in your class.
- The reviewing student should create and insert his or her own comments, and make at least one text change, then send it back to you.
- Once you get the presentation back, review the comments, then make adjustments to the presentation.

**g.** Save the presentation, add your name as the footer on all notes and handouts, check the spelling of the presentation, then view the presentation in Slide Show view.

**h.** Submit your presentation to your instructor, close the presentation, then exit PowerPoint.

# Independent Challenge 3

You are the assistant director of operations at NorthWest Container, Inc., an international marine shipping company based in Seattle, Washington. NorthWest handles 45 percent of all the trade between Asia, the Middle East, and the West Coast of the United States. You need to give a quarterly presentation to the company's operations committee outlining the type and amount of trade NorthWest handled during the previous quarter.

Plan a presentation with at least six slides that details the type of goods NorthWest carries. Create your own content, but assume the following:

- NorthWest hauls automobiles from Tokyo to San Francisco. Northwest can usually haul between 2,800 and 3,500 automobiles in a quarter.
- NorthWest hauls large equipment made by Caterpillar Tractor and John Deere Tractor from the United States.
- NorthWest hauls common household goods that include electronic equipment, appliances, toys, and furniture.
- NorthWest owns 10 cargo ships that can operate simultaneously. All 10 ships were in operation during the last quarter.
- NorthWest hauled a total of 3.8 million tons during the last quarter.

## Independent Challenge 3 (continued)

a. Start PowerPoint, create a new presentation based on a template or theme in the New Presentation dialog box, then save it as **PPT H-NorthWest**.

b. Use the information provided to help develop the content for your presentation. If you have Internet access, use the Internet to research the shipping business.

c. Use at least two different media clips to enhance your presentation.

d. Set transitions and animations, and rehearse slide timings.

e. View the presentation in Slide Show view.

**Advanced Challenge Exercise** *(requires Internet connection and instructor approval)*

- Create a personal Windows Live ID account on the Microsoft Web site.
- Click the Slide Show tab on the Ribbon, then click the Broadcast Slide Show button in the Start Slide Show group.
- Follow the instructions to invite one or more attendees to view the broadcast, then broadcast your presentation.
- End the broadcast.

f. Check the spelling of the presentation, add your name as a footer on all notes and handouts, then save your work.

g. Submit your presentation to your instructor, close the presentation, then exit PowerPoint.

## Real Life Independent Challenge

Your assignment for your American history class is to create a photo album based on your personal life and family history. You must use your own pictures of past and present family members, pets, a family home, a family business, or any other type of family activity that help tell the story of your personal family life and history.

a. Start PowerPoint, create a photo album presentation, insert your pictures to the presentation, then save it as **PPT H-My Family History** to the drive and folder where you store your Data Files.

b. Add your name to the title slide and as the footer on the handouts.

c. Use the Edit Photo Album dialog box to format the pictures. An example of a family photo album is shown in Figure H-21.

d. Check the spelling of the presentation, save your changes, then view the final presentation in Slide Show view.

e. Submit your presentation to your instructor, close the presentation, then exit PowerPoint.

**FIGURE H-21**

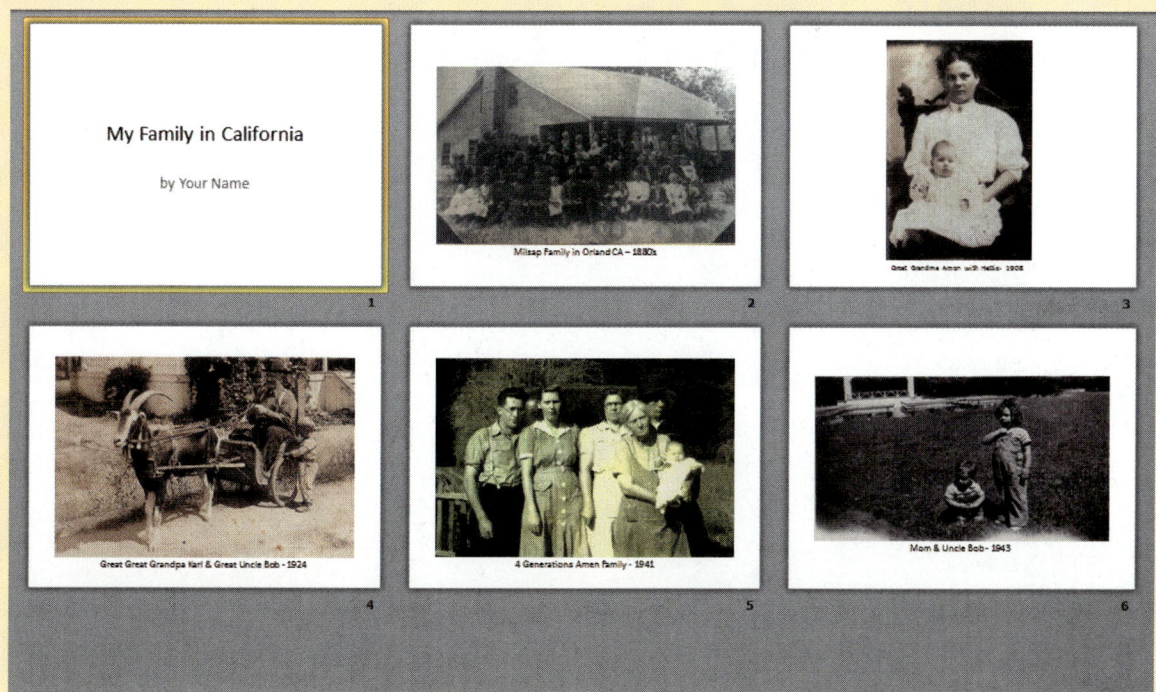

# Visual Workshop

Create the slide shown in Figure H-22. Save the presentation as **PPT H-National Parks**. The SmartArt graphic uses the Vertical Curved List layout. Apply the Insert SmartArt Style, apply a transition to the slide, apply a slide timing of 12 seconds, then apply entrance and exit animations to each object in the SmartArt graphic. Add your name to the slide footer, then submit your presentation to your instructor.

**FIGURE H-22**

# Glossary

**Action button** An interactive button that you click in Slide Show view to perform an activity, such as advancing to the next slide.

**Backstage view** The view that appears when you click the File tab. Use this view to manage a presentation file.

**.bmp** The file extension for the bitmap graphics file format.

**Broadcast** Present a slide show to an audience over the Internet in real time using a Web browser.

**Clip art video** The illusion of making a static object appear to move. Some graphics such as an animated .gif (Graphics Interchange Format) file has motion when you run the slide show.

**Comment** A note you attach to a slide or an object on a slide.

**Compatibility Checker** Finds potential compatibility issues between a PowerPoint 2010 presentation and earlier versions of PowerPoint.

**Destination file** The file an object is embedded into, such as a presentation.

**Digital video** Live action captured in digital format by a movie camera.

**Encryption** A security process that protects a file from unauthorized access by use of a password.

**Error bars** Identify potential error amounts relative to each data marker in a data series.

**File format** A file type, such as .pptx, .bmp, .jpg, or .gif.

**Fixed layout format** A specific file format that locks the file from future change.

**.gif** The file extension for the graphics interchange format.

**graphics format** The type of graphics file, for example, Joint Photographic Experts Group Format (*.jpg), TIFF Tag Image Format (*.tif), or Bitmap (*.bmp).

**Hyperlink** An object or link (a filename, word, phrase, or graphic) that, when clicked, "jumps to" another location in the current file or opens another PowerPoint presentation, a Word, Excel, or Access file, or an address on the World Wide Web.

**.jpg** The file extension for the JPEG (Joint Photographic Experts Group) file format.

**Kiosk** A freestanding booth that can contain a computer used to display information, usually situated in a public area.

**Laser pointer** A pointer you use in Slide Show view to highlight parts of the slide.

**Link** A connection between a source file and a destination file, which when the source file is updated, the destination file can also be updated. Can also refer to a hyperlink.

**Macro** An action or a set of actions that you use to automate tasks.

**Major gridlines** Identify major units on a chart axis.

**Minor gridlines** Identify minor units on a chart axis.

**Narration** A voice recording you make using a microphone on one or more slides. Narrations play during a slide show.

**Photo album** A type of presentation that displays photographs.

**Presenter view** A special view that permits you to run a presentation through two monitors.

**Screenshot** A static picture you take of an open program window and insert on a slide.

**Slide Library** A folder where you store presentation slides for others to access, modify, or use.

**SmartArt text pane** A small text pane attached to a SmartArt graphic where you can enter and edit text.

**Source file** Where an object you create with the source program is saved.

**Source program** The program in which a file was created.

**T**ick mark A small line of measurement that intersects an axis and identifies the categories, values or series of a chart.

**Trendline** A graphical representation of an upward or downward movement in a data series, used to predict future tendencies.

**W**eb server A computer that hosts Web pages.

# Index